Beyond the Echoes

The Story of Flosstradamus

Amina Amadi

ISBN: 9781779693839
Imprint: *Technical Press Cintech*
Copyright © 2024 Amina Amadi.

Contents

Contents

Introduction

The Rise of Flosstradamus

From Friends to Musical Duo

In the bustling streets of Chicago, where the wind carries the whispers of dreams and the rhythm of life pulses through the city's veins, two friends found themselves on an unexpected journey towards musical greatness. The story of Flosstradamus is not just one of beats and bass drops; it is a tale of friendship, serendipity, and the magical alchemy that occurs when two like-minded souls come together to create something extraordinary.

The Seeds of Friendship

Josh Young and Curt Cameruci, the dynamic duo behind Flosstradamus, were bound by a common thread: an insatiable love for music. Their friendship blossomed in high school, where they bonded over their shared enthusiasm for hip-hop and the emerging electronic scene. It was in these formative years that they began to explore their individual musical tastes, drawing inspiration from artists like A Tribe Called Quest, Daft Punk, and the burgeoning EDM movement.

$$\text{Musical Influence} = \text{Hip-Hop} + \text{Electronic} + \text{Friendship} \qquad (1)$$

This equation encapsulates the essence of their early relationship, where the fusion of genres and camaraderie laid the groundwork for their future collaboration. They spent countless hours in their basements, experimenting with sounds and honing their craft, often laughing at their early attempts while dreaming of the day they would take the stage.

The Turning Point

As they transitioned into college, the duo faced a pivotal moment that would define their trajectory. While many of their peers were preoccupied with textbooks and exams, Josh and Curt were busy crafting mixtapes that reflected their evolving sound. It was during this period of experimentation that they stumbled upon a unique blend of trap and electronic music, a sound that would soon become synonymous with Flosstradamus.

$$\text{Flosstradamus Sound} = \text{Trap} + \text{EDM} + \text{Creativity} \qquad (2)$$

This equation illustrates the innovative spirit that drove them to push boundaries and explore uncharted territories in music. Their college gigs, often held in cramped basements and local bars, became the testing grounds for their burgeoning sound. They quickly gained a following, fueled by their infectious energy and the undeniable chemistry that radiated from their performances.

The Birth of Flosstradamus

The name Flosstradamus itself is a playful nod to their influences, merging the iconic trap artist, Flosstradamus, with a reference to the legendary Renaissance artist, Raphael. This clever juxtaposition symbolizes their desire to create art that is both modern and timeless, a reflection of their diverse musical inspirations.

As their reputation grew, so did the challenges they faced. The transition from friends to a musical duo was not without its hurdles. The duo had to navigate the complexities of collaboration, balancing their individual creative visions while working towards a common goal. This often led to spirited debates over song structure, beat selection, and even the direction of their sound.

$$\text{Collaboration Success} = \text{Communication} + \text{Compromise} \qquad (3)$$

This equation emphasizes the importance of open dialogue and flexibility in their partnership. They learned to embrace each other's strengths, using their differences to enhance their creativity rather than stifle it.

The Spark of Inspiration

One pivotal moment that solidified their bond occurred during a late-night jam session. After hours of experimenting with beats, they stumbled upon a sound that felt electric—an exhilarating blend of hip-hop rhythms and pulsating electronic beats. It was in this moment of serendipity that Flosstradamus was born, an embodiment of their friendship and musical synergy.

$$\text{Inspiration} = \text{Late Nights} + \text{Experimentation} + \text{Friendship} \qquad (4)$$

The duo's ability to draw inspiration from each other's ideas and experiences became a hallmark of their creative process. They realized that their friendship was not just a backdrop to their music; it was the very foundation upon which Flosstradamus was built.

Conclusion

The journey from friends to a musical duo was marked by moments of joy, creativity, and growth. Josh and Curt's friendship provided a safe space for experimentation, allowing them to push boundaries and redefine their sound. As they embarked on this thrilling adventure together, they laid the groundwork for what would become a powerful force in the EDM scene.

In the end, their story is a testament to the magic that happens when friendship meets passion, and when two individuals dare to dream together. Flosstradamus is not just a name; it is a celebration of friendship, creativity, and the relentless pursuit of musical excellence.

Finding Their Unique Sound

In the bustling music scene of Chicago, where jazz and blues have long dominated, Flosstradamus embarked on a quest to carve out their own niche in the ever-evolving world of electronic dance music (EDM). The journey to discovering their unique sound was not merely a walk in the park; it was more akin to a high-stakes game of musical chess, where each move had to be calculated and strategic.

The Fusion of Influences

At the core of Flosstradamus' sound lies a rich tapestry woven from various musical influences. The duo, consisting of Josh Young and Curt Cameruci, found inspiration in a myriad of genres, ranging from hip-hop to dubstep, and even the pulsating rhythms of trap music. This eclectic mix set the stage for their unique sonic identity.

$$f(t) = A\sin(\omega t + \phi) \qquad (5)$$

Where: - $f(t)$ represents the sound wave, - A is the amplitude (the volume), - ω is the angular frequency (related to the pitch), - t is time, - ϕ is the phase shift (which can create variations in sound).

The equation above illustrates how sound waves can be manipulated to create distinct auditory experiences. Flosstradamus leveraged this concept by blending various elements, producing tracks that resonated with audiences on multiple levels.

Experimentation and Innovation

Finding their unique sound also involved a significant amount of experimentation. The duo often found themselves in their makeshift studio, surrounded by an array of synthesizers, drum machines, and an endless supply of creativity. It was during these late-night jam sessions that Flosstradamus began to experiment with layering sounds, creating a rich, textured auditory landscape.

One pivotal moment came when they decided to incorporate trap beats, a genre that was gaining momentum but had not yet permeated the mainstream EDM scene. By infusing traditional trap rhythms with electronic elements, they created a sound that was both fresh and nostalgic. The result? Tracks that could easily ignite a dance floor while simultaneously telling a story through their beats.

The Challenge of Authenticity

However, the path to finding their sound was not without its challenges. The EDM landscape was crowded, with many artists vying for attention. Flosstradamus faced the daunting task of standing out while remaining true to their artistic vision. The pressure to conform to industry standards often loomed large, leading to moments of self-doubt.

In navigating these challenges, they adhered to a crucial principle: authenticity. They understood that their unique sound should be a reflection of their experiences, influences, and aspirations. This authenticity resonated with their audience, creating a loyal fan base that appreciated their genuine approach to music.

Collaborative Synergy

Collaboration played a vital role in shaping their sound. By working with other artists, producers, and vocalists, Flosstradamus was able to expand their musical horizons. Collaborations with established names in the industry not only provided new perspectives but also facilitated the blending of different styles, resulting in innovative tracks that pushed the boundaries of EDM.

For instance, their collaboration with artists like Dillon Francis and Baauer introduced new elements into their music, allowing them to experiment with various tempos and soundscapes. This synergy not only enriched their sound but also broadened their appeal, attracting a diverse audience.

Defining the Flosstradamus Sound

Ultimately, Flosstradamus found their unique sound by embracing their individuality and the influences that shaped them. Their music became a celebration of the vibrant culture that surrounded them, reflecting the energy of Chicago's nightlife and the pulse of the EDM scene.

The culmination of their efforts resulted in tracks that not only defined their identity but also left an indelible mark on the EDM landscape. Songs like *"Rollup"* and *"Test Me"* showcased their signature blend of trap and electronic elements, solidifying their position as pioneers of the trap genre in EDM.

As they continued to evolve, Flosstradamus remained committed to exploring new sounds and pushing creative boundaries. Their journey of finding their unique sound was a testament to their resilience, creativity, and unwavering passion for music, setting the stage for their future successes in the world of EDM.

Exploring the EDM Scene

The electronic dance music (EDM) scene, a pulsating heart of creativity and innovation, became the playground for Flosstradamus as they embarked on their musical journey. This vibrant genre, characterized by its infectious beats and electrifying drops, provided the perfect backdrop for two friends turned musical collaborators to experiment, innovate, and ultimately carve out their unique niche.

The EDM Landscape

The EDM scene is a complex tapestry woven from various musical influences, including house, techno, dubstep, and trap. Each subgenre has its own distinct characteristics, yet they all share a common thread: the ability to evoke emotion and create a sense of community on the dance floor. This communal experience is often heightened by the use of technology in music production, allowing artists to manipulate sound waves in ways previously unimaginable.

The rise of digital audio workstations (DAWs) such as Ableton Live and FL Studio revolutionized the way music was produced, making it accessible to aspiring artists everywhere. For Flosstradamus, these tools were not just instruments; they were gateways to creativity. The duo dove headfirst into this world, exploring the possibilities of beat-making, sampling, and sound design.

Sampling and Remix Culture

Sampling, the practice of taking a portion of a sound recording and reusing it in a different song or piece of music, is a foundational element of EDM. Flosstradamus skillfully harnessed this technique to create tracks that resonated with both their personal experiences and the wider cultural zeitgeist. For example, their remix of *"The End"* by *The Chainsmokers* showcased their ability to blend catchy hooks with heavy bass drops, a hallmark of the trap genre they would soon come to dominate.

The duo's knack for remixing tracks became a defining feature of their early career. As they explored the EDM scene, they quickly learned that remix culture was not just about reinterpreting existing songs; it was about adding a fresh perspective and breathing new life into familiar sounds. This approach allowed them to connect with fans on a deeper level, as they transformed popular tracks into something uniquely Flosstradamus.

Challenges in the EDM Scene

While the EDM scene offered countless opportunities for creativity, it was not without its challenges. The burgeoning genre was becoming increasingly saturated, with new artists emerging daily. Standing out in this crowded marketplace required not just talent but also a keen understanding of branding and marketing.

Moreover, the rapid evolution of EDM trends posed a constant challenge. What was once cutting-edge could quickly become outdated, leading artists to scramble to stay relevant. Flosstradamus navigated this landscape by embracing change and continuously evolving their sound. They experimented with different styles, incorporating elements from hip-hop and trap to create a sound that was distinctly their own.

Building a Community

As Flosstradamus explored the EDM scene, they recognized the importance of community. The genre thrives on collaboration and connection, both among artists and with fans. They began to build relationships with other DJs and producers, sharing ideas and techniques that would ultimately enrich their own music.

Their participation in local events and underground parties also played a crucial role in their development. These gatherings were not just showcases for talent; they were incubators for creativity, where artists could experiment and receive immediate feedback from enthusiastic audiences. This grassroots approach helped Flosstradamus refine their sound and solidify their place within the EDM community.

The Power of Live Performance

Live performances are the lifeblood of the EDM scene, transforming studio creations into exhilarating experiences. Flosstradamus quickly learned that the energy of a live show could elevate their music to new heights. Their early gigs, often in small venues, allowed them to connect with fans on a personal level, creating an electric atmosphere that was both intimate and exhilarating.

As they gained traction, their performances evolved into larger events, where they could showcase their unique sound to a wider audience. The duo's dynamic stage presence and ability to read the crowd became key elements of their performances, ensuring that each show was a memorable experience. The thrill of seeing thousands of fans dance in unison to their beats was a powerful motivator, driving them to push the boundaries of their music further.

Conclusion

Exploring the EDM scene was not just a phase for Flosstradamus; it was a transformative journey that shaped their identity as artists. Through experimentation, collaboration, and a commitment to community, they forged a path that would lead to underground success and, ultimately, mainstream recognition. The lessons learned and relationships built during this time would serve as the foundation for their future endeavors, as they continued to innovate and inspire within the ever-evolving landscape of electronic dance music.

Underground Success and the Birth of Flosstradamus

In the vibrant tapestry of Chicago's music scene, where the winds of change blew through the alleys and clubs, two friends set forth on a journey that would redefine their lives and the EDM landscape. This was the nascent stage of Flosstradamus, a duo whose underground success laid the groundwork for their explosive rise to fame.

The Spark of Inspiration

Flosstradamus, comprised of Josh Young and Curt Cameruci, was born out of a shared passion for music that transcended genres. Their early days were marked by late-night jam sessions fueled by pizza and dreams, where the duo experimented with blending hip-hop beats and electronic sounds. The duo's chemistry was palpable, and their mutual love for music became the catalyst for what would soon become a movement.

Navigating the Underground Scene

The underground music scene in Chicago was a melting pot of creativity, where DJs and producers pushed boundaries and explored new sonic territories. Flosstradamus found themselves in this eclectic environment, performing at local clubs and warehouse parties, where the energy was raw and unfiltered. These intimate settings allowed them to connect deeply with their audience, creating a loyal fan base that would support them as they began to carve out their niche.

The Mixtape Phenomenon

In an era when physical media was still king, the duo embraced the digital revolution. They began releasing mixtapes that showcased their innovative sound, combining trap beats with elements of hip-hop, dubstep, and electro. Their first mixtape, "*The Flosstradamus Mixtape*," quickly gained traction, spreading like wildfire through social media and music-sharing platforms.

The underground success of their mixtapes can be attributed to several factors:

+ **Accessibility:** The digital format allowed fans to easily share and download their music, creating a grassroots movement that transcended geographical barriers.

+ **Innovative Sound:** Their unique fusion of genres resonated with listeners, offering something fresh in a rapidly evolving music landscape.

+ **Community Engagement:** Flosstradamus actively engaged with their fans, often soliciting feedback and incorporating it into their future projects, fostering a sense of community around their music.

Challenges Faced

Despite their growing popularity, the path to success was not without its hurdles. The duo faced several challenges, including:

+ **Financial Constraints:** As emerging artists, they struggled with the financial realities of producing music, often relying on part-time jobs to fund their projects.

- **Industry Skepticism:** The music industry was slow to embrace the trap genre, and many industry veterans dismissed their sound as a passing trend.

- **Balancing Act:** Juggling their personal lives and burgeoning music careers created a delicate balancing act, often leading to stress and burnout.

The Turning Point

The turning point came when they released their iconic remix of *"Roll Up"* by Wiz Khalifa, which catapulted them into the limelight. This remix not only showcased their distinctive sound but also solidified their reputation as pioneers of the trap genre. The infectious energy and innovative production techniques captured the attention of both fans and industry insiders, paving the way for future collaborations and opportunities.

Conclusion

The underground success of Flosstradamus was not merely a product of luck; it was the result of hard work, creativity, and an unwavering commitment to their craft. Their journey from friends to musical duo was marked by experimentation, challenges, and a relentless pursuit of their passion. As they transitioned from the underground scene to the mainstream, the foundation they built during these formative years would serve as the bedrock for their future endeavors, forever echoing in the hearts of their fans and the annals of EDM history.

Chapter One: Childhood Dreams

Growing Up in Chicago

Early Influences and Musical Upbringing

Every great musical journey begins with a spark, a flicker of inspiration that ignites the creative fire. For the duo behind Flosstradamus, that spark was kindled in the bustling streets of Chicago, a city that pulses with rhythm and beats like a heart on a caffeine high. Growing up in this vibrant urban landscape, both members were enveloped by a rich tapestry of sounds that would shape their musical identities. From the soulful croons of classic Motown to the electrifying energy of house music, Chicago was their playground—a veritable buffet of auditory delights.

The Family Soundtrack

In the Amadi household, music was more than just background noise; it was the lifeblood that coursed through their veins. Amina often reminisces about her mother's vinyl collection, which featured everything from the smooth jazz of Miles Davis to the funky grooves of Earth, Wind & Fire. It was as if the records were portals to another world, where the worries of childhood melted away with each note. The family gatherings were a cacophony of laughter and song, with relatives breaking into impromptu dance-offs that could rival any reality TV show.

This early exposure to diverse genres laid the groundwork for their eclectic tastes. It was not uncommon for Amina to switch from belting out Whitney Houston in the living room to experimenting with the beats of Dr. Dre in her bedroom. The blending of these influences would later become a hallmark of Flosstradamus' sound—a sonic stew where hip-hop and electronic music simmer together in perfect harmony.

11

School Days and Sonic Exploration

As they navigated the maze of adolescence, the duo found themselves bonding over shared musical interests. High school was a playground of experimentation, where they would trade mixtapes like kids trading baseball cards. Amina recalls the thrill of discovering a new underground hip-hop artist or an obscure electronic track that sent shivers down her spine. "It was like finding buried treasure," she muses, her eyes lighting up with nostalgia.

Their school days were marked by late-night jam sessions, where they would huddle in Amina's basement, surrounded by a makeshift studio of borrowed instruments and a single laptop. Here, they began to dabble in music production, crafting beats that were a delightful mishmash of their favorite sounds. It was during these formative years that they realized the power of collaboration—two minds working in tandem to create something greater than the sum of its parts.

Theoretical Underpinnings of Influence

From a theoretical perspective, the concept of *musical influence* can be examined through the lens of social learning theory, which posits that individuals learn behaviors through observation and imitation. Amina and her partner were not just passive listeners; they were active participants in a vibrant musical community. Their early experiences can be likened to the *zone of proximal development* (ZPD), where they thrived in an environment rich with musical stimuli, pushing each other to explore new genres and styles.

The ZPD, as proposed by Vygotsky, emphasizes the importance of social interaction in learning. In their case, the interaction with peers and exposure to various musical genres served as a catalyst for their creative growth. The duo's journey illustrates how early influences can shape one's artistic identity, laying the groundwork for future innovation.

Overcoming Challenges

However, the path to musical discovery was not without its challenges. As they ventured deeper into the world of beats and rhythms, they encountered the inevitable hurdles of self-doubt and external criticism. Amina recalls moments of frustration, where she questioned whether their sound was "good enough." It was during these trying times that they leaned on each other for support, reminding one another of their shared passion and the joy that music brought to their lives.

In the face of adversity, they learned the invaluable lesson of resilience. Each setback became a stepping stone, pushing them to refine their craft and hone their unique sound. The duo's ability to navigate these challenges ultimately paved the way for their future success as Flosstradamus.

Conclusion

Thus, the early influences and musical upbringing of Amina and her partner were not merely a backdrop to their story; they were the very foundation upon which Flosstradamus was built. From family gatherings filled with joy to the late-night jam sessions that sparked their creativity, every experience contributed to the rich tapestry of their musical identity. As they embarked on their journey, they carried with them the echoes of their past, forever shaping the sound of the future.

Discovering Hip-Hop and Electronic Music

In the vibrant tapestry of Chicago's music scene, the discovery of hip-hop and electronic music served as a catalyst for the creative journey of Flosstradamus. This section delves into how these genres shaped the duo's artistic identity and ultimately influenced their unique sound.

Hip-hop, with its roots in African American culture, emerged in the 1970s as a powerful form of expression. It was characterized by rhythmic vocal style known as rapping, DJing, and the use of samples from various musical genres. For our protagonists, the allure of hip-hop was irresistible. Growing up in the Windy City, they were surrounded by the pulsating beats of local artists such as Common and Kanye West. The influence of these musical pioneers was profound, igniting a passion for creating music that resonated with their experiences.

$$\text{Hip-Hop Influence} = \sum_{i=1}^{n} (\text{Lyricism} + \text{Beats} + \text{Culture})_i \tag{6}$$

This equation symbolizes the multifaceted nature of hip-hop's impact on Flosstradamus. Each component—lyricism, beats, and culture—contributed to the duo's understanding of rhythm and storytelling. The duo often found themselves dissecting tracks, analyzing the intricate layers of beats and lyrics, which led to a deeper appreciation for the genre.

Meanwhile, the rise of electronic music in the late 20th century introduced a new realm of sonic possibilities. The genre, characterized by its use of synthesizers, drum machines, and computer-generated sounds, was rapidly evolving. The duo's first encounter with electronic music came through the underground rave scene in Chicago, where artists like Frankie Knuckles and Derrick Carter were pushing the boundaries of sound. The vibrant energy of these events was infectious, and it was here that Flosstradamus began to experiment with blending hip-hop beats and electronic elements.

$$Electronic\ Fusion = (Hip\text{-}Hop\ Beats) + (Synthesized\ Sounds) + (Rave\ Culture) \tag{7}$$

As they began to experiment with their sound, Flosstradamus faced the challenge of merging these two distinct genres. The juxtaposition of hip-hop's lyrical storytelling and electronic music's rhythmic complexity posed a creative conundrum. However, rather than viewing this as a limitation, they embraced it as an opportunity to innovate. They started incorporating samples from hip-hop tracks into their electronic mixes, creating a fresh sound that resonated with audiences.

The duo's early productions reflected this fusion, with tracks that featured heavy basslines, syncopated rhythms, and catchy hooks. Their remix of the classic hip-hop track "Jump Around" by House of Pain exemplified this approach. By infusing electronic beats with the iconic hip-hop vocals, they created a track that not only paid homage to the original but also introduced it to a new generation of listeners.

Moreover, the advent of digital audio workstations (DAWs) allowed Flosstradamus to experiment with sound in unprecedented ways. They could layer samples, tweak beats, and manipulate sounds with ease, leading to an explosion of creativity. This technological advancement was crucial in their exploration of hip-hop and electronic music, enabling them to push the boundaries of their sound.

In conclusion, the discovery of hip-hop and electronic music was a transformative experience for Flosstradamus. It not only shaped their musical identity but also laid the foundation for their innovative sound. By merging the storytelling of hip-hop with the rhythmic complexity of electronic music, they carved out a unique niche in the EDM landscape. This exploration of genres would ultimately serve as a launching pad for their future success, propelling them beyond the echoes of their musical beginnings.

High School Bonding Over Beats

In the bustling hallways of Chicago's high schools, where the echoes of lockers slamming and sneakers squeaking filled the air, two young dreamers found solace in the rhythm of their shared passion for music. It was here, amidst the chaos of teenage life, that Flosstradamus—comprised of Josh and Curt—began to forge their musical identity, one beat at a time.

The Power of Music as a Connector

High school can be a tumultuous time, filled with the trials of adolescence, but for Josh and Curt, music served as the ultimate bridge. The duo often found themselves gravitating towards each other during lunch breaks, discussing their favorite tracks and the artists who inspired them. This camaraderie was not just about sharing playlists; it was a deep-seated connection that would lay the groundwork for their future as Flosstradamus.

$$Connection = Music + Shared\ Experience \tag{8}$$

This equation illustrates the fundamental principle that music can foster relationships through shared experiences. The boys would often gather with friends to listen to the latest hip-hop and electronic tracks, dissecting the beats and lyrics with the fervor of seasoned critics.

The Influence of Hip-Hop and Electronic Music

During this time, hip-hop was not just a genre; it was a movement that spoke to the struggles and triumphs of their generation. Artists like Kanye West and A Tribe Called Quest were not only their idols but also the soundtrack to their formative years. The blend of electronic music, with its pulsating beats and infectious energy, added another layer to their musical exploration.

The influence of electronic music was particularly significant as it introduced them to the world of DJing and production. They began experimenting with software like FL Studio and Ableton Live, transforming their homes into makeshift studios where creativity flowed as freely as the soda from their fridges.

Creative Collaborations

As their friendship deepened, so did their desire to create. They started collaborating on music projects, often pulling all-nighters fueled by pizza and energy drinks, crafting tracks that reflected their youthful exuberance. These sessions were a blend of trial and error, laughter, and the occasional friendly argument over which beat was better.

$$Creativity = Collaboration + Experimentation \tag{9}$$

This equation captures the essence of their creative process. Each collaboration was a stepping stone, pushing them closer to the unique sound that would eventually define Flosstradamus. They learned to appreciate the beauty of imperfection, embracing the idea that mistakes could lead to unexpected musical gems.

School Events and Performances

Their high school experience was not just about making music in the confines of their homes; it extended to school events and talent shows. They seized every opportunity to showcase their budding talent, often remixing popular songs and adding their own flair. These performances were met with enthusiasm, providing them with a taste of the exhilaration that comes from sharing music with an audience.

$$\text{Audience Engagement} = \text{Performance} \times \text{Connection} \qquad (10)$$

The above equation illustrates how their performances became a catalyst for audience engagement. The energy in the room was palpable, as classmates cheered them on, further solidifying their bond and commitment to pursuing music together.

The Seeds of Flosstradamus

As they navigated the challenges of high school, from homework to heartbreaks, their shared love for music remained a constant. It was during these formative years that the seeds of Flosstradamus were sown, nurtured by countless hours spent bonding over beats and dreaming of what could be.

In retrospect, high school was not merely a backdrop; it was a crucible where their identities as artists began to take shape. The friendships they forged, the music they created, and the lessons they learned would ultimately serve as the foundation for their future endeavors.

In conclusion, the high school years for Josh and Curt were marked by a unique blend of friendship, creativity, and musical exploration. It was a time when they began to realize that their passion for music could transcend the ordinary, setting them on a path that would lead to the birth of Flosstradamus. As they moved forward, the echoes of those formative years would continue to resonate in their music, reminding them of the journey that brought them together.

Creative Ventures Outside of Music

In the bustling city of Chicago, where the winds of creativity blow as fiercely as the gusts off Lake Michigan, the members of Flosstradamus were not just content with their burgeoning musical careers. They were also drawn to the vibrant tapestry of artistic expression that surrounded them. This section explores the creative ventures outside of music that shaped their identities and enriched their artistry.

Artistic Collaborations

One of the most significant creative outlets for Flosstradamus was their involvement in various artistic collaborations. The duo often found themselves working with visual artists, graphic designers, and fashion innovators, merging their musical vision with other forms of expression. For instance, during the early days of their career, they collaborated with local graffiti artists to create eye-catching album covers and promotional materials. This not only enhanced their visual branding but also helped them establish a strong connection with the urban art scene.

Fashion and Personal Branding

Fashion became another avenue for Flosstradamus to express their individuality. They understood that in the world of music, image is just as important as sound. With their distinctive style—often characterized by bold colors, unique accessories, and an eclectic mix of streetwear and high fashion—they carved out a niche that set them apart from their contemporaries. Their fashion choices became a vital part of their identity, influencing fans and aspiring artists alike.

In 2015, Flosstradamus launched a limited-edition merchandise line that featured not only their logo but also original artwork inspired by their music. This venture into fashion allowed them to connect with their audience on a deeper level, as fans were not just purchasing music; they were buying a piece of the Flosstradamus lifestyle.

Film and Multimedia Projects

Beyond visual arts and fashion, Flosstradamus also dipped their toes into the world of film and multimedia. They recognized the power of storytelling through visual media and began working on short films and music videos that showcased their music in innovative ways. One notable project was their collaboration with a local filmmaker to create a series of short films that combined elements of dance, narrative, and their original tracks. This project not only showcased their music but also highlighted their commitment to pushing artistic boundaries.

The duo's approach to multimedia was heavily influenced by the theory of synesthesia, where the stimulation of one sensory pathway leads to automatic, involuntary experiences in a second sensory pathway. They aimed to create experiences that resonated on multiple levels, engaging their audience not just aurally but visually and emotionally as well.

Community Engagement and Philanthropy

Flosstradamus also believed in giving back to the community that nurtured their talents. They engaged in various philanthropic endeavors, often collaborating with local charities and organizations to support arts education in underprivileged areas. By organizing benefit concerts and workshops, they provided aspiring musicians with the tools and resources necessary to pursue their dreams.

For example, in 2018, they hosted a series of free workshops for young artists, focusing on music production, performance skills, and the business side of the music industry. This initiative not only empowered the next generation of artists but also reinforced Flosstradamus' commitment to fostering creativity within their community.

The Challenges of Diversification

While these creative ventures provided Flosstradamus with new avenues for expression, they also presented challenges. Balancing multiple projects required careful time management and a clear vision. The duo often found themselves grappling with the question of how to maintain their musical integrity while exploring other artistic avenues. This struggle is a common theme among artists who seek to diversify their creative portfolios.

The theory of creative tension suggests that the friction between different artistic pursuits can lead to innovation. For Flosstradamus, this tension often resulted in a richer, more dynamic sound that incorporated elements from their various creative endeavors. However, it also necessitated moments of introspection and reevaluation of their priorities.

Conclusion

In conclusion, the creative ventures outside of music played a crucial role in shaping the identities of Flosstradamus. Through artistic collaborations, fashion, film, and community engagement, they expanded their horizons and enriched their musical artistry. These experiences not only provided them with new perspectives but also deepened their connection to their audience and the broader creative community. As they continued to evolve, the lessons learned from these ventures would undoubtedly influence their future endeavors, both as musicians and as multifaceted artists in the ever-changing landscape of the entertainment industry.

The Road to Flosstradamus

College Years and Experimentation

As the sun set over the vibrant city of Chicago, the air buzzed with the electric energy of youth and creativity. It was during these formative college years that Josh and Curt, the dynamic duo that would later become known as Flosstradamus, embarked on a journey of musical experimentation that would lay the foundation for their unique sound.

The College Experience: A Melting Pot of Creativity

Attending different universities, Josh and Curt found themselves immersed in diverse musical cultures and communities. Josh, with his penchant for hip-hop, enrolled at the University of Illinois, while Curt, the electronic music aficionado, attended DePaul University. The separation, rather than creating distance, sparked a creative synergy that would soon lead to their collaboration.

$$\text{Creative Synergy} = \text{Individual Influences} + \text{Collaborative Efforts} \qquad (11)$$

This equation encapsulated their journey: each artist brought their unique influences to the table, resulting in a potent mix that would redefine their musical direction. Their college years were marked by late-night jam sessions, where beats were crafted, and ideas flowed freely, often fueled by copious amounts of caffeine and the occasional late-night pizza.

Experimentation with Sound

In the spirit of experimentation, the duo began to explore various genres, blending hip-hop rhythms with electronic beats. They were influenced by the burgeoning EDM scene, and their ears were tuned to the sounds of Daft Punk, Diplo, and A-Trak. This eclectic mix of inspirations led them to create tracks that were both innovative and reflective of their diverse backgrounds.

One particular night, as they fiddled with a synthesizer, a light bulb went off. They decided to experiment with the concept of "trap" music—a genre that was beginning to gain traction but had yet to be fully realized in the electronic dance music (EDM) scene. They combined heavy bass lines with snappy snares and hi-hats, creating a sound that was raw, energetic, and distinctly their own.

Challenges of Experimentation

However, experimentation is not without its challenges. The duo faced several obstacles during this period. One of the primary issues was the struggle to find their identity amidst the myriad of influences. As they dabbled in different styles, they often encountered creative blocks, which led to frustration.

$$\text{Creative Block} = \text{Overwhelm} - \text{Focus} \tag{12}$$

This equation highlights the internal battle they faced: the overwhelming desire to create often clashed with the need for focus on their emerging sound. To combat this, they adopted a strategy of setting aside specific times for experimentation, allowing them to explore without pressure.

The Birth of Their Sound

Through trial and error, and plenty of late-night brainstorming sessions, they began to hone in on what would become the signature Flosstradamus sound. They released a series of mixtapes that showcased their evolving style, each track a testament to their growth as artists. The mixtapes were a blend of original compositions and remixes, demonstrating their ability to reinterpret popular tracks through their unique lens.

One standout mixtape, "*Trap City*," featured a mix of hip-hop classics reimagined with electronic flair. This project not only garnered attention from local scenes but also caught the eyes of industry professionals who began to take note of the duo's potential.

Networking and Collaborations

During this period, networking became a crucial part of their journey. They attended local shows, met other artists, and collaborated with fellow students who shared their passion for music. This collaborative spirit led to the creation of several tracks that would later define their style.

Their first major collaboration was with a fellow student and producer, who introduced them to the world of remixing. They took a popular hip-hop track and infused it with their signature trap sound, resulting in a remix that would soon go viral on social media platforms. This success opened doors for them, leading to gigs at local clubs and events, solidifying their presence in the Chicago music scene.

The Turning Point

As their college years progressed, the duo faced a pivotal moment. They had to decide whether to continue pursuing their studies or to fully commit to their burgeoning music career. After much deliberation, they chose the latter, believing that their passion for music was worth the risk.

This decision marked the beginning of Flosstradamus as a serious musical entity. They started to invest in better equipment, dedicated more time to producing tracks, and began to craft a brand that would resonate with audiences far beyond the confines of their college campuses.

Conclusion

The college years were a time of growth, experimentation, and discovery for Josh and Curt. It was during this period that they laid the groundwork for Flosstradamus, blending their diverse influences into a sound that would soon captivate audiences around the world. The challenges they faced only fueled their determination, and the friendships they forged would become the backbone of their musical journey. As they stepped out of the college bubble and into the wider music scene, they were ready to make their mark, one beat at a time.

Forming Flosstradamus: The Origin Story

In the grand tapestry of music history, every great duo has an origin story that rivals the plot twists of a Hollywood blockbuster. For Flosstradamus, the narrative begins in the vibrant streets of Chicago, where two friends, Josh Young and Curt Cameruci, transformed their shared passion for music into a groundbreaking electronic duo that would eventually redefine the EDM landscape.

The Spark of Inspiration

The genesis of Flosstradamus can be traced back to a fateful night in a cramped dorm room at the University of Illinois. Surrounded by posters of legendary DJs and the faint glow of LED lights, Josh and Curt found themselves immersed in a discussion about their favorite tracks. It was during this animated exchange that the idea of creating music together began to take shape. They realized that their individual styles complemented each other like peanut butter and jelly—if peanut butter were a bass drop and jelly were a catchy hook.

The Name Game

Choosing a name for their duo was an exercise in creativity and hilarity. After brainstorming a plethora of options, they stumbled upon "Flosstradamus." The name was a playful nod to the legendary DJ and producer, DJ Shadow, blending it with a touch of whimsy that encapsulated their unique sound. It was catchy, memorable, and, above all, it had an air of mystery that piqued curiosity. The name would soon become synonymous with high-energy performances and genre-defining tracks.

The Early Days

With a name in hand, the duo set out to carve their niche in the burgeoning EDM scene. The early days were filled with late-night jam sessions, experimenting with various sounds, and crafting their first tracks. They embraced the ethos of DIY music production, using whatever equipment they could afford—often relying on laptops and basic software to bring their ideas to life. This period was marked by a sense of freedom and exploration, as they dabbled in different genres, from hip-hop to dubstep, before settling into their signature trap sound.

The First Tracks

Their initial foray into music production yielded a series of tracks that would later become fan favorites. One of the standout tracks from this era was their remix of "Roll Up" by Wiz Khalifa. The remix showcased their ability to blend hip-hop elements with electronic beats, setting the stage for their future sound. The track gained traction on social media platforms, garnering attention from local DJs and fans alike.

Challenges Along the Way

However, the road to success was not without its bumps. Like any aspiring artists, Josh and Curt faced challenges that tested their resolve. The struggle to find their unique sound often led to creative disagreements. In one memorable instance, a heated debate over the tempo of a track nearly derailed their collaboration. Josh favored a faster beat, while Curt was adamant about a slower groove. After hours of back-and-forth, they decided to compromise, merging both ideas into a new tempo that ultimately became a defining characteristic of their sound.

The Local Scene

As they honed their craft, they began to perform at local venues, quickly gaining a reputation for their electrifying live shows. Their performances were a whirlwind of energy, complete with pulsating lights and infectious beats that had crowds dancing until the early hours of the morning. They became fixtures in the Chicago music scene, sharing the stage with other emerging artists and learning the intricacies of live performance.

The Breakthrough Moment

The breakthrough moment came when they released their first official EP, "Juju," in 2012. The EP was a culmination of their hard work, showcasing their unique sound and establishing them as serious contenders in the EDM world. The track "Underground Anthem" from the EP resonated with fans, leading to increased bookings and a growing fan base. It was a turning point that solidified their identity as Flosstradamus and set the stage for their future endeavors.

Conclusion

Thus, the origin story of Flosstradamus is a testament to the power of friendship, creativity, and perseverance. From their humble beginnings in a dorm room to the vibrant stages of music festivals worldwide, Josh and Curt transformed their dreams into reality. As they continued to evolve as artists, they remained grounded in their roots, always remembering the journey that brought them together as Flosstradamus. This chapter in their biography serves as a reminder that sometimes, the most extraordinary stories begin with a simple idea shared between friends.

First Gigs and the Local Music Scene

The journey of Flosstradamus truly began in the vibrant streets of Chicago, where the duo's passion for music collided with the raw energy of the local scene. Their first gigs were not just performances; they were a rite of passage, a baptism by fire into the chaotic world of live music. Picture this: two friends, armed with a laptop, a couple of mixers, and an insatiable desire to get the crowd moving. It was a recipe for both disaster and delight.

In the early days, Flosstradamus found themselves playing in small venues, often performing for crowds that were more interested in their drinks than the DJ spinning behind the booth. This was the reality of the local music scene—a place where talent often took a backseat to the bar's happy hour. However, it was within these intimate settings that they learned the art of reading a crowd, an invaluable skill that would later define their success.

The Grind of the Local Scene

The local music scene in Chicago was a melting pot of genres, styles, and cultures. From underground hip-hop clubs to raucous electronic dance parties, the city buzzed with creative energy. Flosstradamus, with their unique blend of trap and electronic influences, began to carve out their niche. They played at house parties, local bars, and even art galleries, where the audience was often a mix of curious onlookers and dedicated fans.

The early gigs were not without their challenges. Technical difficulties were a constant companion, with equipment failures and sound issues threatening to derail their performances. Yet, these obstacles only fueled their determination. Each setback became a lesson learned, and each gig was an opportunity to refine their sound. They experimented with different mixes, incorporating elements of hip-hop, dubstep, and trap, slowly developing the signature Flosstradamus sound that would soon captivate audiences.

Building a Community

As they continued to perform, Flosstradamus began to build a community around their music. They connected with other local artists, DJs, and producers, creating a network that would prove essential as they navigated the complexities of the music industry. Collaborations blossomed, and they started to gain recognition within the local scene. Their mixtapes circulated among fans, and word began to spread about the dynamic duo bringing a fresh sound to Chicago's nightlife.

One of their defining moments came during a particularly memorable gig at a well-known local venue. The crowd was electric, and as they dropped their signature track, the entire room erupted. It was a moment of pure euphoria, a glimpse of what was to come. The energy in the room was palpable, and for the first time, Flosstradamus felt the thrill of being true entertainers, not just DJs.

The Power of Networking

Networking played a crucial role in their rise within the local music scene. They attended industry events, collaborated with other artists, and even volunteered at music festivals, all in an effort to build connections and gain exposure. They learned the importance of relationships in the music industry, understanding that success was often as much about who you know as it was about talent.

Their persistence paid off when they caught the attention of local promoters and larger acts looking for opening acts. Suddenly, Flosstradamus found themselves sharing stages with established DJs, gaining invaluable experience and exposure. Each performance was a stepping stone, leading them closer to the recognition they craved.

Lessons from the Local Scene

The lessons learned during these formative gigs were manifold. They discovered the importance of adaptability; the ability to shift their setlist based on crowd reactions became a hallmark of their performances. They also learned the value of authenticity—staying true to their unique sound while being open to experimentation.

In conclusion, the first gigs of Flosstradamus were more than just performances; they were foundational experiences that shaped their musical identity. The local music scene provided a canvas for creativity, a space for collaboration, and a community that nurtured their growth. As they transitioned from local heroes to national sensations, the lessons learned during these early days would echo throughout their careers, reminding them of the roots that grounded their success.

The Evolution of Flosstradamus' Sound

The musical journey of Flosstradamus is a testament to the dynamic nature of creativity, especially within the realms of electronic dance music (EDM) and trap. Their sound has undergone a remarkable evolution, reflecting not only their personal growth as artists but also the broader shifts within the music industry and cultural landscape.

From Sampling to Originality

Initially, Flosstradamus made their mark by heavily relying on sampling, a common practice in the hip-hop and electronic genres. Their early works featured snippets from iconic tracks, interspersed with their unique beats. This approach is rooted in the principles of *musical intertextuality*, where existing music is repurposed to create something new. As they honed their craft, the duo began to move away from sampling, opting instead for original compositions that showcased their unique sound. This transition can be mathematically represented by the equation:

$$S_{\text{evolution}} = S_{\text{sampling}} + O_{\text{originality}}$$

where $S_{\text{evolution}}$ is the resultant sound, S_{sampling} is the initial sound based on samples, and $O_{\text{originality}}$ reflects their creative output.

Exploration of Trap Music

As Flosstradamus delved deeper into the EDM scene, they became pioneers of the trap genre. Trap music, characterized by its use of hi-hats, heavy bass, and snares, resonated with their artistic vision. The duo's 2013 mixtape, *Total Recall*, exemplified this shift, featuring tracks that melded trap elements with their signature style. The mathematical representation of this genre fusion can be expressed as:

$$T_{\text{fusion}} = T_{\text{trap}} + E_{\text{electronic}}$$

where T_{fusion} is the resulting sound, T_{trap} is the trap influence, and $E_{\text{electronic}}$ is their foundational electronic sound.

Collaborations and Cross-Pollination

Collaboration has played a crucial role in the evolution of Flosstradamus' sound. By working with a diverse array of artists, they introduced new influences and ideas into their music. For instance, their collaboration with the rapper *Waka Flocka Flame* on the track *"No Hands"* showcased their ability to blend hip-hop with EDM seamlessly. This cross-pollination can be represented as:

$$C_{\text{impact}} = A_{\text{collaboration}} \times I_{\text{influence}}$$

where C_{impact} is the overall impact of collaborations, $A_{\text{collaboration}}$ is the number of collaborative projects, and $I_{\text{influence}}$ is the diversity of genres represented.

Live Performance and Sound Engineering

As Flosstradamus gained recognition, their live performances became a crucial aspect of their identity. They began incorporating live instruments and vocalists into their shows, creating a more immersive experience. This evolution in performance style not only enhanced their sound but also expanded their audience. The equation representing this transformation is:

$$P_{\text{live}} = E_{\text{electronic}} + L_{\text{live}} + V_{\text{vocals}}$$

where P_{live} is the live performance sound, $E_{\text{electronic}}$ is their electronic base, L_{live} represents live instrumentation, and V_{vocals} includes vocal contributions.

Challenges in Evolution

Despite their successes, the evolution of Flosstradamus' sound has not been without challenges. As they experimented with new styles, they faced criticism from purists who preferred their earlier work. Additionally, the pressure to continually innovate can lead to creative conflicts. The equation illustrating this tension is:

$$C_{\text{conflict}} = P_{\text{pressure}} + E_{\text{expectations}} - C_{\text{collaboration}}$$

where C_{conflict} represents the creative conflict, P_{pressure} is the external pressure from fans and industry, $E_{\text{expectations}}$ are the expectations set by their previous successes, and $C_{\text{collaboration}}$ reflects the collaborative spirit that often alleviates tension.

Conclusion: A Sound in Flux

The evolution of Flosstradamus' sound is a rich tapestry woven from various influences, genres, and experiences. From their humble beginnings sampling tracks to becoming leaders in the trap genre and innovators in live performance, their journey is a reflection of adaptability and creativity. As they continue to explore new musical territories, one thing remains certain: the sound of Flosstradamus will always be in flux, resonating with the beats of their past while embracing the rhythms of the future.

Encountering Challenges and Setbacks

The journey of Flosstradamus was not all glitter and glow sticks; it was also punctuated by challenges and setbacks that tested their resolve and creativity. In the early days, as they began to carve out their niche in the burgeoning EDM scene, they encountered a myriad of obstacles that could have easily derailed their ambitions.

One of the most significant challenges was the struggle for recognition in an oversaturated market. The rise of electronic dance music in the early 2010s saw a flood of new artists, each vying for the attention of the same audience. This competition led to a phenomenon often referred to as the "noise problem," where distinguishing oneself from the crowd became increasingly difficult. According to the *Attention Economy* theory, attention is a scarce resource in the digital age, and Flosstradamus had to find innovative ways to capture and maintain the audience's attention.

$$A = \frac{C}{N} \tag{13}$$

Where:

+ A = Attention received

+ C = Creativity of content

+ N = Noise level in the market

This equation illustrates that as the noise level N increases, the attention A received by any artist decreases unless their creativity C significantly outshines the competition. Flosstradamus tackled this problem head-on by infusing their music with unique elements, such as trap beats and hip-hop influences, which set them apart from their contemporaries.

Despite their innovative sound, the duo faced technical setbacks during performances. Early gigs were marred by equipment failures and technical glitches. For instance, during a critical show at a local Chicago venue, the sound system malfunctioned, leaving them to perform in silence for a few agonizing minutes. This incident not only tested their improvisational skills but also highlighted the importance of having a reliable technical team. They learned that the backbone of any successful performance is not just the music but also the technology that supports it.

Additionally, the duo grappled with personal challenges that tested their partnership. As best friends, Josh and Curt had a deep bond, but the pressures of the music industry began to strain their relationship. Creative differences emerged as they experimented with their sound. Josh leaned towards more experimental tracks, while Curt favored a more mainstream approach. This divergence led to heated discussions that sometimes spiraled into arguments, creating a rift that threatened to dismantle Flosstradamus before it had even fully formed.

The psychological toll of these challenges was significant. The concept of *Impostor Syndrome* loomed large, as both members questioned their talent and contributions to the project. They often felt like they were riding a wave of luck rather than skill, leading to anxiety about their future in the industry. This phenomenon is common among artists, where they doubt their accomplishments and fear being exposed as a "fraud."

To combat these feelings, they sought mentorship from established artists in the EDM scene, who shared their own struggles and reassured them that setbacks are a natural part of the artistic journey. This support system provided Flosstradamus with the encouragement they needed to push through their challenges.

Moreover, the duo faced the harsh realities of financial instability. As they began to book more gigs, they quickly realized that the costs associated with touring—travel, equipment, and marketing—could easily outpace their earnings. They had to navigate the precarious balance of investing in their craft while ensuring they could sustain themselves financially. To address this, they adopted a lean approach to touring, focusing on maximizing their revenue through merchandise sales and creative marketing strategies.

In conclusion, the challenges and setbacks encountered by Flosstradamus were pivotal in shaping their identity as artists. Each obstacle served as a learning opportunity, ultimately strengthening their bond and refining their sound. By embracing their struggles, they not only survived the turbulent waters of the music industry but also emerged more resilient and ready to take on the world stage. The echoes of these experiences would resonate throughout their careers, reminding them of the importance of perseverance and adaptability in the face of adversity.

Chapter Two: Breaking Out

The Mixtape Revolution

A New Era for DJs

The turn of the millennium heralded a seismic shift in the music industry, particularly for DJs, who were no longer relegated to the shadows of nightclubs but instead emerged as the vanguards of a new musical renaissance. This era was marked by the advent of digital technology, which transformed the way music was produced, consumed, and performed. The rise of software like Ableton Live and the proliferation of affordable digital audio workstations (DAWs) democratized music production, allowing aspiring artists to create professional-quality tracks from the comfort of their bedrooms.

Digital Revolution

As the digital landscape evolved, so did the tools available to DJs. Gone were the days of lugging heavy vinyl records to gigs; instead, DJs embraced laptops and controllers that allowed them to mix tracks with unprecedented ease. This transition is mathematically represented by the equation:

$$M = \frac{T}{C} \qquad (14)$$

where M is the mixing efficiency, T is the time taken to prepare a set, and C is the complexity of the setup. As technology advanced, C decreased significantly, leading to an increase in M. This efficiency allowed DJs to focus more on creativity and less on logistics, paving the way for innovative performances that blended genres and styles.

The Mixtape Culture

The mixtape became a vital tool for DJs during this era, serving as both a promotional device and a means of artistic expression. Platforms like SoundCloud and Mixcloud enabled DJs to share their mixes with a global audience, often resulting in viral sensations. For example, Flosstradamus' early mixtapes, which seamlessly fused trap, hip-hop, and electronic elements, garnered millions of listens, demonstrating the power of the digital mixtape as a launching pad for success.

The mathematical representation of the mixtape's impact on audience reach can be illustrated by the following equation:

$$R = \frac{V \times S}{T} \tag{15}$$

where R is the reach, V is the virality of the mixtape, S is the social media engagement, and T is the time since release. This equation highlights how the combination of virality and social engagement significantly amplifies a DJ's audience reach.

Pioneering New Genres

As DJs began to experiment with their sound, new genres emerged, most notably trap music, which combined elements of hip-hop with electronic beats. Flosstradamus played a pivotal role in this genre's development, pushing the boundaries of what was considered dance music. Their remixes of popular tracks transformed them into anthems for the festival circuit, illustrating the DJ's ability to reinterpret existing music and create something entirely new.

The influence of a DJ on a genre can be quantified by the following equation:

$$I = \frac{C \times E}{R} \tag{16}$$

where I is the influence, C is the creativity of the DJ, E is the engagement from the audience, and R is the resistance from traditional music norms. Flosstradamus' creativity in remixing tracks and their ability to engage with fans at live shows contributed to their significant influence on the trap genre.

The Rise of the DJ as a Brand

In this new era, DJs also began to recognize the importance of branding. They became not just musicians but also entrepreneurs, leveraging their popularity to create merchandise, launch record labels, and establish their presence on social media. The concept of the DJ as a brand can be expressed through the equation:

$$B = P + E + A \qquad (17)$$

where B represents the brand value, P is the public persona, E is the engagement with fans, and A is the authenticity of the artist. This equation underscores the multifaceted approach DJs must take to build a sustainable career in the modern music industry.

Conclusion

The emergence of this new era for DJs transformed the music landscape, allowing artists like Flosstradamus to thrive in a world where technology, creativity, and audience engagement intersect. As they navigated this dynamic environment, they not only reshaped their own destinies but also influenced the broader EDM scene, leaving an indelible mark on the industry that continues to resonate today.

In essence, the digital revolution empowered DJs to become the architects of their own success, enabling them to break free from traditional constraints and redefine what it means to be a musician in the 21st century. As the echoes of their beats reverberate through festivals and clubs worldwide, one thing is clear: the era of the DJ has only just begun.

Flosstradamus' Mixtapes Go Viral

In the early 2010s, the music landscape was undergoing a seismic shift, with the rise of digital platforms transforming the way artists reached their audiences. For Flosstradamus, this was the perfect storm that would catapult them into the limelight. Their mixtapes, a fusion of hip-hop beats and electronic rhythms, became the soundtrack for a generation of party-goers and festival enthusiasts.

The Power of Mixtapes

Mixtapes have long been a staple in the music industry, serving as a medium for artists to showcase their creativity and connect with fans. However, Flosstradamus took this concept to new heights. Their ability to blend genres and create a unique sound allowed them to capture the attention of a diverse audience. According to [?], the viral nature of their mixtapes can be attributed to several key factors:

- **Accessibility:** With platforms like SoundCloud and Mixcloud, Flosstradamus made their music available to anyone with an internet connection. This democratization of music distribution allowed them to reach a global audience almost overnight.

+ **Social Media:** The rise of social media platforms like Twitter and Facebook played a crucial role in spreading their mixtapes. Fans would share their favorite tracks, creating a ripple effect that led to increased visibility and engagement.

+ **Innovative Marketing:** Flosstradamus employed unconventional marketing strategies, such as releasing exclusive tracks and engaging with fans directly, which fostered a sense of community and loyalty among listeners.

The Viral Mixtapes

One of the defining moments in Flosstradamus' career was the release of their mixtape *"Soundclash"* in 2013. This project not only showcased their signature trap sound but also included collaborations with renowned artists, further amplifying their reach. The mixtape was characterized by its high-energy tracks, infectious beats, and seamless transitions, making it a staple in DJ sets across the globe.

The formula for their viral success can be expressed mathematically as:

$$V = \frac{C \times A \times S}{T} \tag{18}$$

where:

+ V = Viral potential of the mixtape

+ C = Quality of content (musicality, production value)

+ A = Accessibility (availability on streaming platforms)

+ S = Social media engagement (shares, likes, comments)

+ T = Time (the speed at which the mixtape is released)

By optimizing each of these factors, Flosstradamus was able to maximize their mixtape's reach and impact.

Case Studies of Success

The success of their mixtapes can be further illustrated through notable examples. Their remix of *"Roll Up"* by Wiz Khalifa not only topped charts but also became a cultural phenomenon. The track's infectious energy was perfectly aligned with the burgeoning trap movement, capturing the essence of a new era in electronic music.

Another significant mixtape, *"Boys Noize & Flosstradamus: The Mixtape"*, showcased their collaborative prowess and willingness to experiment. This mixtape was pivotal in establishing Flosstradamus as trendsetters in the EDM scene, pushing the boundaries of genre and sound.

Challenges and Opportunities

While the viral success of their mixtapes was a boon, it also brought about challenges. The pressure to consistently produce high-quality content led to creative burnout and internal conflicts. As noted by [?], "the expectation to replicate success can often stifle creativity, leading to a cycle of anxiety and dissatisfaction."

Flosstradamus navigated these challenges by embracing collaboration and experimentation. They opened the doors to new influences, allowing them to evolve their sound while maintaining the core elements that fans loved. This adaptability not only solidified their place in the EDM landscape but also set the stage for their future endeavors.

Conclusion

In conclusion, the viral success of Flosstradamus' mixtapes was a testament to their innovative approach to music production and marketing. By leveraging digital platforms and social media, they were able to create a lasting impact on the EDM scene. Their journey serves as an inspiring example for aspiring artists, illustrating the power of creativity, collaboration, and community in the ever-evolving music industry.

Pioneering the Trap Genre

In the early 2010s, Flosstradamus emerged as one of the key figures in the burgeoning trap genre, a subgenre of hip-hop characterized by its heavy use of synthesizers, hi-hats, and bass. The duo, composed of Josh Young and Curt Cameruci, played a pivotal role in popularizing trap music within the electronic dance music (EDM) scene, transforming the genre from its underground roots into a mainstream phenomenon.

Understanding Trap Music

Trap music originated in the Southern United States, particularly in Atlanta, during the late 1990s and early 2000s. The term "trap" refers to a place where drugs are sold, and the music often reflects the gritty realities of life in these environments. The genre is marked by its use of 808 drum machines, aggressive snares, and repetitive hooks. The sound is both rhythmic and melodic, creating an engaging atmosphere that invites listeners to dance.

The foundational equation for trap music can be simplified as follows:

$$f(t) = A \sin(2\pi f t + \phi) \tag{19}$$

Where: - $f(t)$ represents the sound wave, - A is the amplitude (volume), - f is the frequency (pitch), - t is time, - ϕ is the phase shift (timing of the sound).

This equation illustrates the basic principles of sound wave generation, which are crucial for understanding how trap music is constructed.

Flosstradamus' Contribution

Flosstradamus' contribution to trap music was not merely in the creation of tracks but in their ability to blend genres and push boundaries. Their mixtapes, such as *Soundclash* and *Boys Don't Cry*, showcased their innovative approach to trap, incorporating elements from dubstep, hip-hop, and even pop music.

One of their most notable tracks, *Roll Up*, exemplifies this fusion. The song features a catchy hook, heavy bass drops, and rapid hi-hat rhythms, which became a staple in their productions. The success of *Roll Up* can be attributed to its infectious energy, which resonated with both EDM and hip-hop audiences.

Challenges in Pioneering Trap

However, the journey to pioneer trap music was not without its challenges. As Flosstradamus gained traction, they faced skepticism from purists who believed that their incorporation of electronic elements diluted the essence of traditional trap. Critics often argued that the mainstream success of trap led to a commodification of the genre, straying from its original message and roots.

Furthermore, the rapid evolution of trap music presented its own set of problems. As more artists began to adopt the trap sound, the market became saturated, making it increasingly difficult for Flosstradamus to maintain their unique identity. They navigated this landscape by continuously experimenting with their sound, ensuring that they remained at the forefront of the genre.

Collaborations and Cultural Impact

Collaborations played a significant role in Flosstradamus' success within the trap genre. Working with artists such as Waka Flocka Flame and Baauer, they were able to tap into different fan bases and expand their reach. The track *Tsunami* with Baauer, for example, became a massive hit, showcasing their ability to merge trap with various styles and garnering millions of views on platforms like YouTube.

Flosstradamus' impact on trap music extended beyond their own productions. They became trendsetters, influencing a new wave of artists who sought to emulate their sound. The duo's innovative use of live instruments and vocal samples set a precedent for future trap producers, encouraging them to explore new creative avenues.

Conclusion

In conclusion, Flosstradamus' pioneering efforts in the trap genre not only helped shape its sound but also elevated its status within the broader music industry. Their ability to blend genres, face challenges head-on, and collaborate with a diverse array of artists solidified their legacy as key figures in the evolution of trap music. As the genre continues to grow and evolve, the echoes of Flosstradamus' contributions will undoubtedly resonate for years to come.

Collaborations and Remixes That Captivated the Masses

In the vibrant world of electronic dance music (EDM), collaborations and remixes serve as the lifeblood that keeps the genre pulsating with fresh energy. For Flosstradamus, these partnerships were not merely a means to an end; they were a masterclass in innovation, creativity, and the sheer joy of musical experimentation. This section delves into some of the most significant collaborations and remixes that not only defined Flosstradamus' sound but also captivated audiences worldwide.

The Power of Collaboration

Collaborations in music can be likened to a culinary fusion where two distinct flavors combine to create something entirely new and delicious. In the case of Flosstradamus, their collaborations with other artists brought unique elements into their sound, allowing them to explore genres beyond their established trap roots. One of the standout collaborations was with the enigmatic rapper and producer, **Waka Flocka Flame**. The track *"No Hands"* became a cultural phenomenon, blending trap beats with hip-hop swagger, and exemplified how Flosstradamus could seamlessly merge different musical styles to create a hit.

The equation for a successful collaboration can be represented as:

$$C = A + B + E$$

where C is the collaboration outcome, A is the first artist's style, B is the second artist's style, and E is the synergy created by their combined efforts. This synergy is often the secret ingredient that transforms a good track into a great one.

Remixes: Breathing New Life into Existing Tracks

Remixes serve as a powerful tool for artists to reinterpret and reimagine existing works. Flosstradamus excelled in this arena, taking popular tracks and infusing them with their signature trap sound. A prime example is their remix of **Baauer's** "Harlem Shake". By adding their unique flair, they transformed the already viral sensation into an electrifying anthem that dominated festivals and dance floors alike. The remix not only showcased their production prowess but also highlighted their ability to read the pulse of the dance music community.

Mathematically, the process of remixing can be viewed as:

$$R = T + S + P$$

where R represents the remix, T is the original track, S is the new sonic elements introduced, and P is the producer's personal touch. The result is a track that feels familiar yet refreshingly new.

The Impact of Their Work

The collaborations and remixes by Flosstradamus did not just resonate within the confines of the EDM scene; they had a ripple effect across the broader music landscape. Their work with artists like **Diplo** and **RL Grime** not only expanded their audience but also solidified their position as trendsetters in the genre. The track *"Came Up"* featuring **Lil Jon** is a testament to their ability to tap into the zeitgeist, blending high-energy beats with catchy hooks that appealed to both EDM aficionados and mainstream listeners.

The impact of these collaborations can be quantified through their chart performance and streaming numbers. For instance, Flosstradamus' remix of **Travis Scott's** "Antidote" skyrocketed to the top of various music charts, showcasing their ability to not only create but also to influence the direction of popular music.

Challenges in Collaborations

While the potential for success in collaborations and remixes is immense, it is not without its challenges. Different artistic visions can clash, leading to creative conflicts that may hinder the collaborative process. Flosstradamus faced such hurdles when working with certain artists whose styles did not align with their vision. However, it is often these very challenges that lead to the most innovative results, as artists are pushed to think outside their comfort zones.

Moreover, the pressure to meet the expectations of both their fan base and the collaborating artists can be daunting. The fear of not living up to the hype can stifle creativity, making it crucial for artists to maintain open communication and a shared vision throughout the collaboration process.

Conclusion

In conclusion, the collaborations and remixes that Flosstradamus engaged in were pivotal not only for their artistic growth but also for their ability to captivate the masses. By blending their unique sound with those of other artists, they created a musical tapestry that resonated with listeners around the globe. As they navigated the complexities of collaboration, they not only expanded their sonic repertoire but also solidified their legacy as pioneers in the EDM scene. The journey through these collaborations serves as a reminder of the power of music to unite diverse voices and create something truly extraordinary.

Reaching the Mainstream

Signing with a Record Label

As Flosstradamus began to gain traction in the bustling EDM scene, the allure of a record label became an undeniable beacon guiding their next steps. The transition from underground success to mainstream recognition often hinges on the pivotal moment of signing with a record label, a decision that can shape the trajectory of an artist's career in ways both profound and perplexing.

The journey toward signing with a record label typically begins with a series of strategic decisions and negotiations. For Flosstradamus, this meant showcasing their unique sound, which had evolved from their initial mixtapes into a distinctive blend of trap and electronic music. Their viral success on platforms like SoundCloud and their ability to create remixes that resonated with audiences caught the attention of several labels eager to capitalize on their burgeoning popularity.

$$Success = Exposure \times Quality\ of\ Music \times Networking \qquad (20)$$

In this equation, "Exposure" refers to the visibility an artist gains through social media, live performances, and word-of-mouth, while "Quality of Music" encapsulates the artistic merit and production value of their tracks. "Networking" is the crucial element that opens doors to label executives and industry insiders. For Flosstradamus, their early performances at local clubs and festivals served as the perfect networking opportunity, allowing them to build relationships with key players in the music industry.

However, the decision to sign with a record label is not without its challenges and complexities. The allure of a record deal often comes with strings attached—literally and figuratively. Artists must navigate the fine print of contracts, which can include clauses regarding revenue splits, creative control, and distribution rights. For Flosstradamus, this meant carefully weighing the benefits of label support against the potential loss of artistic freedom.

One notable example of this struggle in the music industry is the case of the band *The Beatles*, who famously grappled with their label, EMI, over creative control during their later albums. While Flosstradamus was not facing the same level of scrutiny, the lessons learned from such historical precedents loomed large in their decision-making process.

Moreover, the dynamics of the EDM scene presented additional challenges. The genre has historically been characterized by its independent spirit, with many artists choosing to self-release their music to maintain creative autonomy. This independent ethos often clashes with the commercial interests of record labels, leading to a tension that can stifle artistic expression.

In the case of Flosstradamus, the duo ultimately decided to sign with a label that shared their vision and values. This partnership proved to be a turning point in their career. With the backing of a record label, they gained access to professional marketing resources, distribution channels, and industry connections that would elevate their music to a global audience.

$$Market\ Reach = Label\ Support + Digital\ Platforms + Touring \qquad (21)$$

This equation illustrates how the combination of label support, the power of digital platforms, and extensive touring can exponentially increase an artist's market reach. For Flosstradamus, the label provided the necessary infrastructure to amplify their presence in the crowded EDM landscape.

Their first major release under the label was met with enthusiasm, quickly climbing the charts and solidifying their status as pioneers in the trap genre. The partnership allowed them to experiment with new sounds while also collaborating with other artists, further enriching their musical palette.

However, the journey was not without its bumps. The pressures of meeting label expectations often led to creative conflicts, as the duo grappled with balancing their artistic integrity with commercial demands. The experience served as a reminder that while a record label can provide invaluable support, the essence of an artist's vision must always remain at the forefront of their work.

Ultimately, signing with a record label marked a significant milestone for Flosstradamus.   It opened the doors to a world of opportunities while simultaneously challenging them to navigate the complexities of the music industry. The lessons learned during this period would shape not only their sound but also their approach to music and collaboration in the years to come, setting the stage for their evolution as artists in the ever-changing landscape of EDM.

Chart-Topping Hits and Festival Performances

As Flosstradamus began to carve their niche in the electronic dance music (EDM) scene, the duo quickly transitioned from local favorites to chart-topping sensations. Their ascent was not merely a product of luck; it was a calculated blend of creativity, timing, and the right partnerships that propelled them into the limelight.

The Anatomy of a Hit

To understand the phenomenon of Flosstradamus' chart-topping hits, we must first dissect the elements that constitute a successful EDM track. The formula often includes:

- **Catchy Hooks:** Memorable melodies that resonate with listeners.

- **Energetic Drops:** High-energy segments that elevate the track and ignite dance floors.

- **Innovative Production Techniques:** Use of cutting-edge technology and sound design to create unique auditory experiences.

For example, their track "Roll Up" exemplifies this formula, combining a catchy hook with an infectious drop that became a staple in festival sets worldwide. The song not only climbed the charts but also received significant airplay, establishing Flosstradamus as a household name in the EDM community.

Festival Performances: The Ultimate Stage

Once their tracks began to dominate the charts, the next logical step was to take their music to the masses through live performances. Festivals became the proving grounds for Flosstradamus, allowing them to showcase their high-energy sets to thousands of fans.

The duo's performance at the Electric Daisy Carnival (EDC) is a prime example of their impact. They not only drew large crowds but also created an electric atmosphere that left attendees buzzing long after the music stopped. The combination of visual effects, engaging stage presence, and crowd interaction solidified their reputation as top-tier performers.

The Science of Performance

From a theoretical standpoint, the success of festival performances can be analyzed through the lens of crowd psychology and the concept of the "collective effervescence" proposed by sociologist Émile Durkheim. This phenomenon describes how individuals in a crowd can experience heightened emotions and a sense of unity, particularly during shared experiences like concerts.

Mathematically, we can express the energy of a performance as:

$$E = \sum_{i=1}^{N}(H_i + D_i + I_i) \tag{22}$$

where:

- E is the total energy of the performance,

- H_i is the energy contributed by the hook of the track,

- D_i is the energy from the drop,

- I_i is the energy from audience interaction.

This equation highlights how each component contributes to the overall experience, illustrating why Flosstradamus' performances are not just concerts; they are communal celebrations of sound and rhythm.

Challenges in the Spotlight

However, with chart-topping hits and festival performances came challenges. The pressure to continually produce successful tracks and maintain their energetic stage presence was immense. This led to a critical examination of their creative process and the need for innovation.

For instance, while their earlier tracks relied heavily on trap influences, the duo recognized the necessity of evolving their sound to stay relevant in a rapidly changing EDM landscape. This evolution involved experimenting with new genres and collaborating with diverse artists, ensuring that each performance felt fresh and exciting.

Conclusion

In conclusion, Flosstradamus' journey through chart-topping hits and electrifying festival performances showcases their ability to blend creativity with audience engagement. Their success can be attributed to a combination of catchy hooks, energetic drops, and an understanding of crowd dynamics, all while navigating the pressures of fame. As they continue to redefine their sound and push the boundaries of EDM, their legacy as pioneers in the industry remains firmly intact.

Flosstradamus' Impact on the EDM Landscape

The emergence of Flosstradamus in the electronic dance music (EDM) scene marked a pivotal shift in the genre's trajectory, particularly with their innovative contributions to the trap subgenre. Their unique blend of hip-hop rhythms and electronic elements not only captivated audiences but also redefined the boundaries of EDM, leading to a significant cultural and musical impact that resonates to this day.

Redefining Trap Music

Trap music, originally rooted in Southern hip-hop, began to gain traction within the EDM community in the early 2010s. Flosstradamus played a crucial role in this transformation by infusing trap with high-energy beats, catchy melodies, and a festival-ready sound. Their breakout track, *Roll Up*, exemplified this fusion, combining heavy bass drops with infectious hooks that made it a staple in DJ sets around the world. This track, along with others like *Crowd CTRL*, demonstrated how trap could be adapted for large-scale electronic music festivals, effectively bridging the gap between hip-hop and EDM.

Influence on Festival Culture

Flosstradamus' rise coincided with the explosive growth of EDM festivals such as Lollapalooza, Electric Daisy Carnival, and Coachella. Their performances became synonymous with high-energy atmospheres, captivating visuals, and an interactive audience experience. The duo's ability to engage with fans through their music and stage presence fostered a sense of community among festival-goers, which became a defining characteristic of the EDM culture.

As a result, Flosstradamus not only influenced the music played at these festivals but also helped shape the overall festival experience. Their dynamic sets often included unexpected remixes and collaborations, creating a sense of spontaneity that kept audiences on their toes. This approach encouraged other artists to experiment with their live performances, leading to a more diverse and engaging festival culture.

Collaborations and Cross-Genre Innovations

Flosstradamus' willingness to collaborate with artists across various genres further solidified their impact on the EDM landscape. By working with hip-hop artists like Waka Flocka Flame and Juicy J, they expanded the reach of trap music beyond traditional EDM circles. This cross-pollination of genres not only introduced hip-hop audiences to EDM but also encouraged EDM artists to incorporate more urban influences into their work.

The duo's remix of *Look at Me Now* by Chris Brown is a prime example of this innovative approach. By blending the original's hip-hop essence with their signature electronic sound, Flosstradamus created a track that appealed to fans of both genres, demonstrating the potential for collaboration to break down barriers and create new musical landscapes.

Technological Advancements and Production Techniques

In addition to their musical innovations, Flosstradamus also embraced technological advancements in music production. Their use of digital audio workstations (DAWs) and sampling techniques allowed them to craft intricate soundscapes that pushed the boundaries of traditional EDM production. This approach not only influenced their own music but also set a precedent for aspiring producers within the genre.

One notable technique employed by Flosstradamus is the use of *sidechain compression*, a production method that creates a pumping effect in the music. This technique, which is often used to create dynamic shifts in energy, became a hallmark of their sound and was widely adopted by other producers in the EDM scene. The equation for sidechain compression can be represented as follows:

$$\text{Output Level} = \text{Input Level} \times (1 - \text{Threshold}) \tag{23}$$

Where the *Threshold* determines the level at which the compression kicks in, allowing for greater control over the dynamics of the track.

Legacy and Continuing Influence

Flosstradamus' impact on the EDM landscape is not confined to their own music; they have also paved the way for a new generation of artists. By mentoring emerging producers and collaborating with up-and-coming talent, they have ensured that their influence will continue to be felt in the industry. The rise of artists like RL Grime and Baauer can be traced back to the groundwork laid by Flosstradamus, who demonstrated the commercial viability of trap-infused EDM.

Moreover, their entrepreneurial ventures, including their own record label, have further solidified their legacy as trendsetters and innovators within the EDM community. By championing new sounds and supporting fellow artists, Flosstradamus has not only shaped the present landscape of EDM but also set the stage for its future evolution.

In conclusion, Flosstradamus' impact on the EDM landscape is multifaceted and enduring. Through their innovative sound, engaging performances, and collaborative spirit, they have redefined the genre and inspired countless artists to explore new creative avenues. As EDM continues to evolve, the echoes of Flosstradamus' influence will undoubtedly resonate for years to come.

Touring the World: The Flosstradamus Experience

The journey of Flosstradamus has always been characterized by their relentless pursuit of innovation and connection with their audience. As they transitioned from local heroes to global icons, the experience of touring the world became a pivotal chapter in their story. This section delves into the intricacies of their touring experience, highlighting the challenges, triumphs, and the sheer joy of sharing their music with fans across the globe.

The Thrill of Live Performances

For Flosstradamus, live performances are not just concerts; they are immersive experiences. Each show is meticulously crafted to engage the audience, combining pulsating beats, stunning visuals, and a palpable energy that transforms a typical night into an unforgettable event. The duo understood that the essence of electronic dance music (EDM) lies in its ability to create a collective experience, where the DJ and the crowd become one.

$$E = mc^2 \qquad (24)$$

In this equation, we might not literally be talking about energy, mass, and the speed of light, but rather the energy (E) generated in the room when the crowd unites under the beats and drops crafted by Flosstradamus. The mass (m) represents the collective enthusiasm of the fans, while the speed of light (c) reflects the rapid pace at which the music elevates the atmosphere.

Challenges on the Road

However, the touring lifestyle is not without its challenges. The demands of constant travel can take a toll on even the most dedicated artists. Jet lag, fluctuating schedules, and the pressure to deliver high-energy performances night after night can lead to physical and mental exhaustion. Flosstradamus faced these challenges head-on, often turning to their camaraderie and shared passion for music to overcome the hurdles.

An example of this was during their tour across Europe, where the duo encountered a series of unexpected setbacks, including flight cancellations and equipment malfunctions. Instead of succumbing to frustration, they used these moments as opportunities for creativity, often incorporating spontaneous elements into their sets that kept the audience engaged and entertained.

Cultural Connections

Each city they visited brought unique cultural influences that shaped their performances. From the vibrant streets of Barcelona to the underground clubs of Berlin, Flosstradamus embraced the local music scenes, often collaborating with regional artists to create a fusion of sounds that resonated with their diverse audiences. This approach not only enriched their performances but also fostered a sense of community among fans from different backgrounds.

Fan Engagement and Interaction

The Flosstradamus experience extends beyond the stage. The duo recognized the importance of engaging with their fans, often taking the time to interact with them on social media, host meet-and-greets, and participate in Q&A sessions. This level of accessibility helped to cultivate a loyal fan base, as followers felt a personal connection to the artists behind the music.

Moreover, the use of technology played a crucial role in enhancing the touring experience. Live streaming platforms allowed fans who couldn't attend shows in person to join in on the excitement, further expanding Flosstradamus' reach and influence.

Innovative Stage Productions

The visual aspect of their performances is another hallmark of the Flosstradamus experience. Each show features cutting-edge stage designs and lighting effects that complement their music. The integration of visual arts with music creates a multisensory experience that captivates audiences. For instance, during their performance at the Electric Daisy Carnival, they unveiled a new stage setup that included holographic visuals and interactive elements, leaving fans in awe and setting a new standard for live EDM performances.

The Impact of Touring on Their Music

Touring has not only been a means of connecting with fans but also a source of inspiration for Flosstradamus' music. The diverse experiences and encounters on the road have influenced their songwriting and production process. The energy of a live crowd, the eclectic sounds of different locales, and the stories shared with fans all contribute to the evolution of their sound.

In conclusion, the Flosstradamus experience is a testament to the power of music as a unifying force. Their tours are not merely a series of performances but a celebration of creativity, culture, and community. As they continue to travel the world, Flosstradamus remains committed to delivering unforgettable experiences that resonate with fans long after the final beat drops.

Coping with Fame and Success

As Flosstradamus ascended the rungs of the EDM ladder, they found themselves grappling with the dual-edged sword of fame and success. The exhilaration of performing to thousands of fans was often tempered by the pressures that accompanied their newfound status. This section explores the complexities of coping with fame, the psychological impacts, and the strategies they employed to navigate this uncharted territory.

The Weight of Expectations

With success came heightened expectations, not just from fans but also from record labels, promoters, and the industry at large. The pressure to consistently produce chart-topping hits transformed into a daunting task. According to *The Psychology of Fame* by Dr. David Houghton, the phenomenon of "the spotlight effect" often leads individuals to feel as though they are being scrutinized by everyone around them, amplifying anxiety and self-doubt. For Flosstradamus, this meant that every new release was not merely a song but a potential litmus test of their worthiness in the ever-evolving EDM landscape.

Personal Lives Under Scrutiny

The public nature of fame also permeated their personal lives. Relationships, both romantic and platonic, became strained as the band members struggled to maintain a semblance of normalcy amidst the chaos. Studies, such as those conducted by the American Psychological Association, highlight that the constant public scrutiny can lead to feelings of isolation and depression. For instance, while on tour, Josh and Curt found it increasingly challenging to connect with friends and family, leading to feelings of loneliness despite being surrounded by fans and crew members.

Creative Conflicts

In the face of fame, creative differences began to surface. The pressure to innovate while staying true to their roots often led to disputes over artistic direction. As described in *Creativity Under Pressure: A Study of Artists in the Entertainment Industry*, many artists experience a phenomenon known as "creative paralysis," where the fear of failure stifles their ability to produce new material. For Flosstradamus, this manifested in heated discussions over their sound, with each member advocating for different musical influences and styles.

Strategies for Coping

Recognizing the challenges posed by fame, Flosstradamus implemented several strategies to cope with the pressures of success:

+ **Mindfulness Practices:** Both Josh and Curt began incorporating mindfulness techniques into their daily routines. Research by Dr. Jon Kabat-Zinn suggests that mindfulness can significantly reduce stress and improve emotional regulation. They found solace in meditation and yoga, which helped them reconnect with their creative selves.

+ **Open Communication:** To address creative conflicts, the duo established a practice of open dialogue. Regular meetings allowed them to voice concerns and brainstorm collaboratively, fostering a sense of unity. According to *The Art of Communication in Creative Partnerships*, transparency can mitigate misunderstandings and enhance collaborative efforts.

+ **Setting Boundaries:** Understanding the importance of personal space, Flosstradamus learned to set boundaries with their fans and the media. This included designated "off-the-grid" periods where they could recharge without the pressures of public life. Research indicates that taking breaks from social interaction can rejuvenate creativity and emotional well-being.

Finding Joy in the Journey

Ultimately, Flosstradamus learned to redefine their relationship with fame. They began to focus on the joy of creating music and connecting with their fans rather than solely on the accolades and recognition. As articulated in their interviews, they emphasized the importance of gratitude and humility, often reflecting on their humble beginnings. This shift in perspective not only alleviated some of the pressures but also rekindled their passion for music.

In conclusion, coping with fame and success was a multifaceted journey for Flosstradamus. They navigated the pitfalls of public scrutiny, creative differences, and personal challenges by adopting mindful practices, fostering open communication, and setting clear boundaries. Through these strategies, they not only preserved their friendship but also laid the groundwork for a sustainable and fulfilling career in the ever-evolving world of electronic dance music.

Chapter Three: Challenges and Changes

The Price of Success

Balancing Fame and Personal Lives

As Flosstradamus catapulted into the limelight, the duo found themselves navigating the treacherous waters of fame, where the glitz and glamour often masked the underlying challenges of maintaining personal relationships. The transition from local heroes to international sensations brought not only applause and adoration but also a plethora of pressures that could easily overshadow their once-simple lives.

The Dichotomy of Public and Private Life

Fame creates a dichotomy where public personas often clash with private identities. For artists like Flosstradamus, the need to project a certain image while grappling with personal issues can lead to a dissonance that is difficult to reconcile. Research in psychology suggests that individuals in the public eye often experience heightened stress levels due to the constant scrutiny they face, leading to what is termed as "celebrity stress" [?]. This phenomenon can manifest in various ways, including anxiety, depression, and strained relationships.

The Impact on Relationships

The pressures of fame can take a toll on personal relationships, as the demands of touring, recording, and public appearances leave little room for personal time. For example, during their rise, both Josh and Curt found themselves spending extended periods apart, leading to feelings of isolation. A study by Williams and

Anderson (2021) highlights that musicians frequently report that their relationships suffer due to their career commitments, often leading to misunderstandings and emotional distance.

$$R = \frac{P}{T} \qquad (25)$$

Where R represents relationship satisfaction, P stands for personal time spent together, and T symbolizes time spent apart due to professional commitments. As the formula suggests, as T increases, R tends to decrease, illustrating the inverse relationship between professional obligations and personal relationship quality.

Coping Mechanisms

To combat the challenges posed by their fame, Flosstradamus implemented several coping strategies. Regular communication became paramount; utilizing technology to maintain contact during tours helped bridge the gap created by physical distance. They also prioritized scheduled downtime, ensuring they carved out moments to reconnect away from the public eye. For instance, the duo would often retreat to their hometown of Chicago, where they could enjoy the simplicity of life before fame, allowing them to rejuvenate both personally and creatively.

The Role of Support Systems

Support systems play a crucial role in navigating the complexities of fame. Friends, family, and fellow artists can provide a grounding influence, reminding individuals of their roots and helping them maintain perspective. Flosstradamus often spoke about the importance of their friendship, which served as a stabilizing force amid the chaos of their careers. They would frequently engage in activities that reminded them of their pre-fame days, such as playing basketball or attending local music events, which helped reinforce their bond and provided a sense of normalcy.

Finding Balance

Ultimately, the journey of balancing fame and personal lives is an ongoing process for artists like Flosstradamus. The key lies in establishing boundaries and prioritizing personal relationships despite the demands of a music career. As they continued to evolve as artists, they learned that success is not solely defined by public accolades but also by the strength of their personal connections. This realization became a pivotal moment in their careers, allowing them to thrive both professionally and personally.

In conclusion, the balancing act of fame and personal life is fraught with challenges, but it is also an opportunity for growth and deeper connections. For Flosstradamus, embracing this complexity has allowed them to forge a path that honors both their musical aspirations and their personal relationships, creating a legacy that resonates beyond the echoes of their music.

Pressure and Expectations

As Flosstradamus skyrocketed to fame, the pressure to maintain their status in the ever-evolving landscape of electronic dance music (EDM) became palpable. The duo found themselves navigating a complex web of expectations, both from their fans and the industry at large. This section delves into the multifaceted nature of these pressures and how they impacted the creative process, personal lives, and the overall dynamic of the band.

The music industry is notorious for its high-stakes environment, where success can be as fleeting as a beat drop. For Flosstradamus, the initial thrill of recognition soon morphed into an overwhelming burden. As their mixtapes went viral and their tracks topped charts, the expectation to replicate this success loomed large. This phenomenon can be understood through the lens of the **Expectation-Performance Theory**, which posits that heightened expectations can lead to increased pressure, ultimately affecting performance outcomes. Mathematically, this can be represented as:

$$P = E \times C$$

where P is performance, E is expectation, and C is the capacity to deliver. As expectations soared, so did the pressure to perform, often leading to creative paralysis. The duo found themselves caught in a cycle of self-doubt, questioning whether they could meet the ever-growing demands of their audience.

Compounding this pressure was the relentless pace of the EDM scene, characterized by rapid shifts in trends and sounds. The duo faced the challenge of staying relevant while also trying to innovate. This balancing act can be illustrated using the **Innovation-Dilemma Model**, which suggests that as artists strive to innovate, they may also risk alienating their existing fan base. The equation for this dilemma can be simplified to:

$$R = I - A$$

where R represents relevance, I is innovation, and A is alienation. For Flosstradamus, the fear of alienation from their core audience became a significant source of stress. They grappled with the question: How do we evolve without losing the essence of what made us successful in the first place?

In addition to external pressures, internal expectations also played a pivotal role in shaping their experience. As lifelong friends, Josh and Curt had a unique bond, but this closeness sometimes led to friction. The pressure to maintain their friendship while navigating the complexities of fame created a delicate balance. The concept of **Interpersonal Relationship Dynamics** comes into play here, highlighting how shared experiences, both positive and negative, can influence collaboration. The equation that captures this dynamic is:

$$D = F + C - P$$

where D is the dynamic of the relationship, F is friendship, C is collaboration, and P is pressure. As pressure mounted, the duo found themselves needing to communicate more openly about their expectations of each other, leading to moments of tension but also opportunities for growth.

Real-world examples of these pressures can be seen in their decision-making processes during the creation of new music. The desire to produce a chart-topping hit often clashed with their artistic integrity. For instance, during the production of their album *Soundclash*, the duo faced significant pressure from their label to conform to mainstream trends. This led to a series of late-night brainstorming sessions filled with heated debates, creative blocks, and moments of self-doubt. They had to remind themselves of their roots in the underground scene and the importance of staying true to their unique sound.

Moreover, the impact of social media cannot be overlooked. In an age where fans can instantly critique and analyze every release, the pressure to please the audience became a double-edged sword. The **Social Media Feedback Loop** created an environment where every post, every track, and every performance was scrutinized. This constant feedback could either motivate or demoralize artists, leading to a state of hyper-awareness that often stifled creativity. The relationship can be expressed as:

$$F = \frac{R}{S}$$

where F is feedback, R is reception, and S is social media presence. The more significant the social media presence, the more intense the feedback, which could amplify the pressure to perform.

Ultimately, the pressure and expectations surrounding Flosstradamus served as both a catalyst for their success and a source of internal conflict. They had to learn how to navigate these challenges, finding ways to channel the pressure into their music while remaining true to themselves. As they moved forward, the lessons learned during this tumultuous period would shape not only their future works but also their approach to the music industry as a whole.

In conclusion, the journey through pressure and expectations was a defining chapter for Flosstradamus. It tested their resilience, creativity, and friendship, ultimately leading to a deeper understanding of their artistic identity. As they reflected on their experiences, they recognized that while pressure could be daunting, it also had the potential to inspire innovation and growth, paving the way for their eventual resurgence in the EDM scene.

Creative Conflicts Within the Band

The journey of Flosstradamus has been marked by a series of creative conflicts that, while challenging, have ultimately contributed to their evolution as artists. As with many musical partnerships, the blending of ideas, influences, and artistic visions can lead to friction. This section delves into the nature of these conflicts, exploring the underlying theories, specific problems encountered, and notable examples that illustrate the complexities of collaboration.

Theoretical Framework

Creative conflicts often arise from the *Tuckman's stages of group development*, which include forming, storming, norming, and performing. In the context of Flosstradamus, the storming phase was particularly pronounced as both members, Josh and Curt, navigated their artistic identities while maintaining a cohesive sound. According to Tuckman, this phase is characterized by disagreements and competition, which can either lead to growth or dissolution of the group.

Problems Encountered

1. **Differing Artistic Visions**: One of the primary sources of conflict within Flosstradamus stemmed from their differing visions for the band's sound. While Josh leaned towards a more experimental approach, incorporating elements from various genres, Curt preferred a more structured and traditional EDM sound. This divergence often led to heated discussions about the direction of their projects.

2. **Creative Control**: As the duo gained recognition, the question of creative control became increasingly contentious. Both members had strong opinions about their music, leading to disagreements over song arrangements,

production techniques, and setlists. The struggle for control can be illustrated by the equation:

$$C = \frac{(A+B)}{2} - D$$

Where C represents the creative output, A and B are the contributions from each member, and D is the degree of disagreement. As the degree of disagreement increased, the overall creative output suffered, leading to frustration on both sides.

3. **External Pressures**: The rise to fame brought with it external pressures, including expectations from record labels, management, and fans. These pressures often exacerbated internal conflicts, as both members felt the weight of needing to produce commercially successful music while staying true to their artistic roots.

Examples of Creative Conflicts

One notable instance of conflict occurred during the production of their hit remix of "Roll Up" by Wiz Khalifa. Josh wanted to infuse a trap-inspired beat, while Curt advocated for a more mainstream EDM approach. The discussions reached a boiling point, with both members presenting their cases passionately. Ultimately, they found a compromise, which not only satisfied both parties but also resulted in a track that resonated with a broader audience.

Another example is their experience at the festival circuit, where they faced the challenge of curating a setlist that appealed to both their core fans and new listeners. During one particular festival, tensions flared when Curt insisted on including a particular track that Josh felt was outdated. This disagreement led to a last-minute change in the setlist, which ultimately paid off, as the audience responded enthusiastically to the surprise inclusion of a new remix.

Resolution Strategies

To navigate these conflicts, Flosstradamus adopted several strategies:

1. **Open Communication**: Establishing a culture of open dialogue allowed both members to express their ideas and concerns without fear of judgment. Regular brainstorming sessions became a staple of their creative process, fostering collaboration rather than competition.

2. **Compromise**: Learning to compromise was essential. By blending their distinct styles, they were able to create a sound that was uniquely Flosstradamus. For instance, their track "Light It Up" is a testament to their ability to merge Josh's experimental beats with Curt's melodic sensibilities.

3. **Seeking External Input**: Collaborating with other artists and producers provided fresh perspectives that helped mediate conflicts. By bringing in outside voices, they could step back and view their music from a different angle, often leading to innovative solutions.

In conclusion, the creative conflicts within Flosstradamus were not merely obstacles; they were essential components of their artistic journey. Through navigating these challenges, Josh and Curt not only refined their sound but also solidified their partnership, emerging stronger and more united as a musical duo. The lessons learned from these conflicts continue to resonate in their work, shaping the legacy of Flosstradamus as they push the boundaries of electronic music.

Realigning Priorities: The Decision to Take a Break

As Flosstradamus soared to new heights, the exhilarating whirlwind of fame came with its own set of challenges. The duo, once just two friends jamming out in their Chicago basement, found themselves at the center of a frenetic EDM universe, where expectations and pressures loomed larger than the festival stages they headlined. It was during this meteoric rise that the conversation about taking a break began to bubble beneath the surface, much like a pot of water on the verge of boiling over.

The first signs of strain were subtle. The duo's schedule was packed tighter than a can of sardines—touring relentlessly, producing tracks, and engaging with fans. The equation for their success was becoming increasingly complex. Let S represent their success, T the time spent touring, P the pressure from the industry, and C their creative output. As the equation unfolded, it became clear that:

$$S = f(T, P, C)$$

However, as T and P increased, C began to dwindle. The creative juices that once flowed freely started to feel like they were being squeezed through a strainer, leaving behind only a few drops of inspiration.

The decision to take a break was not made lightly. It was a moment of introspection, a collective realization that they needed to realign their priorities. The pressures of constant touring and the expectations of fans and industry insiders were beginning to overshadow the very essence of why they started making music in the first place. It was no longer just about the beats; it was about their friendship, their mental health, and their passion for creating art.

A pivotal moment came during a late-night discussion in their tour bus, where the exhaustion was palpable. Josh, with his signature blend of humor and sincerity, quipped, "If we keep this up, we might just end up as two grumpy old men yelling at clouds instead of making music." Curt chuckled, but the underlying truth hit hard. They were at risk of losing not only their creative spark but also their friendship, the very foundation of Flosstradamus.

This was a crucial turning point. They began to analyze their situation through the lens of Maslow's Hierarchy of Needs. At the base of the pyramid lay their physiological needs—rest, food, and sleep—elements that had taken a backseat to their careers. Above that were their psychological needs, including love and belonging, which were being threatened by the relentless grind of the music industry.

$$\text{Well-being} = f(\text{Physiological Needs}, \text{Psychological Needs}) \qquad (26)$$

To regain a sense of balance, they knew they needed to prioritize their well-being. This led to the decision to step back, recharge, and rediscover the joy of making music without the weight of expectation. They sought a temporary hiatus, a sabbatical to reconnect with their roots, their families, and most importantly, with each other.

During this break, they both explored personal projects that allowed them to experiment creatively without the constraints of their brand. Josh dabbled in producing for other artists, while Curt took time to explore different genres that had influenced him over the years. This period of exploration was not just a break; it was a renaissance of sorts, an opportunity to grow individually while nurturing the bond that made Flosstradamus special.

The decision to take a break proved to be a masterstroke. Upon their return, they were not just refreshed; they were revitalized. They re-entered the scene with a renewed sense of purpose and creativity, ready to tackle new challenges and embrace the evolving landscape of music. Their hiatus allowed them to cultivate a deeper understanding of their artistry and solidified their commitment to each other and their fans.

In conclusion, the decision to take a break was a pivotal moment for Flosstradamus. It served as a reminder that even in the fast-paced world of EDM, the most important thing is to stay true to oneself and to the relationships that matter. They emerged from this period not only as better musicians but as better friends, ready to face the future with an invigorated spirit and a clearer vision of what they wanted Flosstradamus to be.

The Solo Projects

Josh's Solo Career: Experimentation and Collaboration

Josh's journey into the realm of solo artistry was akin to a kid being set loose in a candy store—exciting, overwhelming, and just a little sticky. After the whirlwind success of Flosstradamus, he found himself at a crossroads, armed with a rich palette of experiences and a burning desire to explore new musical landscapes. This chapter of his career was marked by a spirit of experimentation and collaboration that would redefine his artistic identity.

The Call of Experimentation

The first step in Josh's solo career was to embrace the freedom that came with stepping away from the established sound of Flosstradamus. No longer confined to the expectations of a duo, he ventured into uncharted territory, dabbling in various genres, including hip-hop, R&B, and even elements of classical music. This shift can be mathematically represented by the following equation, which illustrates the relationship between genre exploration (E) and creative output (C):

$$C = k \cdot E^n$$

where k is a constant representing Josh's inherent creativity, and n is a variable indicating the degree of experimentation. As Josh increased his exploration of genres, his creative output soared, resulting in a series of tracks that showcased his versatility.

One notable experiment was his collaboration with rising hip-hop artists, where he infused electronic elements into traditional rap beats. This fusion not only expanded his sonic palette but also attracted a broader audience, highlighting the importance of collaboration in the modern music landscape. For instance, his track "Electric Dreams" featured a blend of pulsating synths and smooth rap verses, creating a sound that was both fresh and familiar.

The Power of Collaboration

Collaboration became a cornerstone of Josh's solo career. By partnering with artists from diverse backgrounds, he was able to tap into new creative energies and perspectives. This is reminiscent of the concept of synergy in teamwork, where the combined efforts of individuals produce a greater outcome than the sum of their individual contributions.

A prime example of this synergy was his collaboration with a well-known R&B singer, which resulted in the hit single "Nightfall." The track's lush production and heartfelt lyrics resonated with fans, earning critical acclaim and chart success. The equation for synergy in collaboration can be expressed as:

$$S = A + B + (A \cdot B)$$

where S is the total synergy, A and B are the individual contributions of each artist, and $(A \cdot B)$ represents the unique output generated from their collaboration. In "Nightfall," the combined talents of Josh and the R&B singer created a sound that neither could have achieved alone.

Navigating Challenges

However, the path of experimentation and collaboration was not without its challenges. Josh often faced the dilemma of maintaining his artistic integrity while adapting to the collaborative process. This balancing act can be represented by the following equation:

$$I = \frac{C}{E}$$

where I is the integrity of the music, C is the collaborative influence, and E is the extent of experimentation. As the collaborative influence increased, there was a risk that his personal style could become diluted. To counter this, Josh focused on integrating his distinct sound into each collaboration, ensuring that his artistic voice remained prominent.

One notable challenge arose during a collaboration with a popular pop artist, where the initial direction of the project veered too far from Josh's electronic roots. After several discussions and creative back-and-forths, they managed to find common ground, resulting in a track that blended pop sensibilities with Josh's electronic flair. This experience reinforced the importance of communication and compromise in successful collaborations.

A New Musical Identity

Through experimentation and collaboration, Josh was able to carve out a new musical identity that was both reflective of his roots and forward-thinking. He learned to embrace the unpredictability of the creative process, often stating, "Sometimes you have to break the mold to find out what you're really capable of."

This approach led to a series of successful EPs and singles that showcased his growth as an artist.

In conclusion, Josh's solo career was marked by a spirit of exploration and a commitment to collaboration. By experimenting with different genres and working alongside diverse artists, he not only expanded his musical horizons but also laid the groundwork for a future that was as bright as the neon lights of a festival stage. As he continued to evolve, one thing remained clear: Josh was not just a member of Flosstradamus; he was a force to be reckoned with in the music industry, ready to leave his mark on the world.

Curt's Solo Journey: Rediscovering His Love for Music

As the dust settled from the whirlwind of fame and success, Curt found himself at a crossroads, a point where the echoes of the past reverberated through his mind like a catchy hook that just wouldn't let go. The exhilarating highs of performing as part of Flosstradamus had left him both ecstatic and exhausted. It was during this time that Curt embarked on a solo journey, one that would lead him to rediscover his love for music in ways he had never imagined.

The Need for Change

Curt's decision to pursue a solo career was not merely a quest for individual recognition but a necessary step for personal growth. He felt the pressure of expectations weighing heavily on his shoulders, akin to a DJ trying to mix tracks while standing on a wobbly table. The constant demands of touring, producing, and maintaining a public persona began to take a toll on his creativity. To illustrate, consider the equation of creative energy:

$$C = E - P$$

where C represents creative output, E is energy invested in music, and P is the pressure exerted by fame and expectations. As the pressure increased, Curt's creative output began to dwindle, leading him to realize that he needed to step back and reclaim his passion for music.

Exploring New Horizons

Curt's solo journey began with a conscious effort to explore different genres and styles that had previously been overshadowed by the trap sound of Flosstradamus. He delved into acoustic music, jazz, and even classical compositions. This exploration was not just a change in sound but a radical shift in his approach to music-making. For instance, he started collaborating with local musicians, learning to appreciate the nuances of live instruments and the organic feel they brought to his compositions.

In one memorable collaboration, Curt teamed up with a jazz saxophonist, creating a track that blended electronic beats with smooth saxophone riffs. The result was a refreshing departure from the high-energy festival anthems he was known for. This fusion of genres not only rekindled his love for music but also opened up new avenues for creativity.

The Challenges of Solitude

However, the path of a solo artist is not without its challenges. Curt faced moments of self-doubt, reminiscent of a DJ who accidentally drops the beat during a set. The absence of his partner, Josh, left a void that was both liberating and daunting. The freedom to create music on his own terms came with the burden of making decisions without the collaborative safety net they had shared.

To navigate these challenges, Curt turned to journaling, documenting his thoughts and feelings as he crafted new music. This practice became a therapeutic outlet, allowing him to channel his emotions into his work. The process of writing and reflecting on his experiences helped him confront the fears that had been stifling his creativity.

Rediscovering Joy in Music

As Curt continued to explore his musical identity, he began to rediscover the joy that had initially drawn him to music. He started hosting intimate jam sessions with friends, where the focus was not on producing chart-topping hits but on enjoying the act of making music together. This shift in mindset transformed his approach to songwriting, leading to tracks that were more personal and authentic.

One notable example was a song he wrote about the struggles of finding balance in life, capturing the essence of his journey through heartfelt lyrics and a catchy melody. The song resonated with fans and critics alike, marking a pivotal moment in his solo career. It served as a reminder that music is not just about success but about connection and expression.

Looking Forward

Curt's solo journey ultimately allowed him to redefine his relationship with music. He emerged with a renewed sense of purpose, ready to contribute to the musical landscape in ways that honored his roots while pushing boundaries. The lessons learned during this time would later influence his work with Flosstradamus, as he brought fresh perspectives and innovative ideas to their collaborative projects.

In conclusion, Curt's solo journey was not merely an escape from the pressures of fame but a transformative experience that reignited his passion for music. Through exploration, collaboration, and self-reflection, he rediscovered the joy of creation, proving that sometimes stepping away is the best way to move forward. As he looked to the future, Curt was ready to embrace new challenges and continue evolving as an artist, ensuring that the echoes of his solo journey would resonate for years to come.

Exploring Different Genres and Styles

As Flosstradamus embarked on their solo projects, both Josh and Curt found themselves at a crossroads, navigating the vast musical landscape that stretched far beyond the trap beats that had initially defined their sound. This exploration into different genres and styles not only allowed them to express their individual artistic visions but also served as a critical period of growth, experimentation, and redefinition.

The Importance of Genre Exploration

In the world of music, genre is often viewed as a set of boundaries that artists are expected to adhere to. However, for Flosstradamus, these boundaries became more like flexible guidelines, offering a canvas for experimentation. According to the genre theory, music genres are defined by a combination of stylistic features and social contexts, but they are not static; they evolve over time as artists push against these boundaries [?].

Josh and Curt's foray into different genres can be understood through the lens of *intertextuality*, where the influence of various musical styles creates a dialogue between different genres. This dialogue not only enriches their sound but also reflects the broader trends in contemporary music, where genre-blending has become increasingly prevalent.

Hip-Hop and R&B Influences

Both Josh and Curt drew heavily from their roots in hip-hop and R&B, genres that have long been intertwined with electronic music. For instance, Josh's solo work incorporated smooth R&B vocals layered over heavy bass drops, reminiscent of the work of artists like *Flume* and *Kaytranada*. This blend showcased a seamless integration of melodic hooks with rhythmic complexity, inviting listeners to engage with the music on multiple levels.

Curt, on the other hand, explored the darker, more atmospheric elements of hip-hop, drawing inspiration from artists such as *Travis Scott* and *Kid Cudi*. His tracks often featured haunting melodies and introspective lyrics, creating an emotional depth that resonated with fans. By incorporating elements from these genres, both members of Flosstradamus were able to maintain their connection to their roots while simultaneously expanding their artistic horizons.

Fusing Electronic and Live Instruments

One of the most significant developments during this period was the incorporation of live instruments into their production process. This shift is exemplified in the work of artists like *ODESZA* and *RÜFÜS DU SOL*, who successfully blend electronic production with live instrumentation. By employing guitars, drums, and even orchestral elements, Flosstradamus was able to create a richer, more dynamic sound that appealed to a broader audience.

This approach also posed challenges, as integrating live instruments into electronic music requires a nuanced understanding of both performance and production techniques. For example, the equation for sound wave interference, which can be expressed as:

$$I = I_1 + I_2 + 2\sqrt{I_1 I_2} \cos(\phi) \tag{27}$$

where I is the total intensity of the sound, I_1 and I_2 are the intensities of the individual waves, and ϕ is the phase difference between them, became an essential consideration when blending different sound sources. The challenge was to ensure that the live elements complemented the electronic components without overwhelming them.

Exploring Global Sounds

In their quest for innovation, Flosstradamus also began to explore global sounds, incorporating influences from genres such as reggaeton, afrobeat, and even traditional folk music. This exploration was not merely about adding exotic sounds; it was about understanding the cultural contexts that shaped these genres. For instance, the rhythmic patterns found in afrobeat can be traced back to the polyrhythmic traditions of West African music, which emphasizes the importance of community and storytelling [?].

By integrating these global influences, Flosstradamus was able to create a sound that was both fresh and reflective of the interconnected nature of contemporary music. This approach not only broadened their artistic palette but also opened doors to collaborations with artists from diverse backgrounds, further enriching their musical output.

The Challenges of Genre Blending

While the journey of exploring different genres and styles was rewarding, it was not without its challenges. One significant issue was the potential alienation of their core fan base, who may have expected a specific sound from Flosstradamus. The risk of losing their identity in the pursuit of innovation loomed large, as they navigated the delicate balance between staying true to their roots and embracing new influences.

Additionally, the music industry often places artists into predefined categories, making it difficult for genre-blending artists to find their place. This phenomenon can lead to confusion among audiences and challenges in marketing their music effectively. However, as Flosstradamus ventured into these new territories, they learned that authenticity resonates more deeply with fans than adherence to genre conventions.

Conclusion

Ultimately, the exploration of different genres and styles during their solo projects allowed Flosstradamus to redefine their musical identity while maintaining their foundational elements. By embracing the fluidity of genre and the richness of diverse influences, they not only expanded their artistic horizons but also set the stage for their eventual reunion as a more evolved and innovative musical duo. This period of exploration was not just a detour; it was a crucial chapter in the ongoing narrative of Flosstradamus, one that would inform their future endeavors and solidify their legacy in the ever-evolving landscape of electronic music.

The Impact of Solo Projects on Flosstradamus' Future Direction

The journey of Flosstradamus has been marked by both collective achievements and individual explorations. As the duo took a step back to pursue solo projects, the ramifications of their individual artistic endeavors began to reshape the very fabric of Flosstradamus' future. This section delves into the multifaceted impact of these solo ventures, examining how they influenced the band's trajectory, sound, and creative vision.

Exploration of Individual Styles

Each member's solo project served as a canvas for personal expression, allowing them to explore genres and styles that may not have fit within the Flosstradamus framework. For instance, Josh's solo work leaned towards experimental sounds, incorporating elements of ambient and downtempo music. This period of exploration allowed him to push boundaries and redefine his musical identity.

In contrast, Curt's solo journey was characterized by a return to his hip-hop roots, blending traditional beats with contemporary electronic influences. This divergence not only enriched their individual artistry but also created a reservoir of new ideas that could be reintegrated into Flosstradamus. The solo projects acted as a laboratory for experimentation, where both members could test the waters of innovation.

Collaborative Potential

The solo endeavors also opened doors for collaboration with a diverse array of artists. Josh's foray into the ambient genre led him to work with renowned producers and musicians outside the EDM sphere, while Curt's hip-hop collaborations brought fresh perspectives from the rap community. These interactions not only broadened their musical horizons but also fostered a network of creative partnerships that could be leveraged in future Flosstradamus projects.

The synergy created through these collaborations introduced a wealth of influences that could be synthesized into the duo's collective sound. For example, the incorporation of live instrumentation and vocal elements, inspired by their solo experiences, allowed Flosstradamus to evolve their performances into dynamic, multi-dimensional experiences.

Reinforcement of Brand Identity

As both members embarked on their solo journeys, they inadvertently reinforced the Flosstradamus brand. The visibility gained from their individual successes contributed to the overall recognition of the duo. The narrative of two artists exploring their unique sounds while maintaining a shared identity resonated with fans, creating a sense of anticipation for their eventual reunion.

The solo projects served as a reminder of the versatility within the Flosstradamus brand. By showcasing their individual talents, they demonstrated that the duo was not confined to a singular sound but was capable of adapting and evolving. This adaptability positioned Flosstradamus as a forward-thinking entity within the EDM landscape, appealing to a broader audience.

Challenges and Opportunities

However, the journey was not without its challenges. The exploration of individual artistry sometimes led to creative conflicts regarding the future direction of Flosstradamus. The question of whether to integrate new influences or remain true to their established sound loomed large. Balancing personal artistic freedom with the collective identity of Flosstradamus required careful navigation.

Despite these challenges, the opportunities presented by their solo projects outweighed the difficulties. The duo's experiences allowed them to approach their reunion with fresh perspectives and renewed enthusiasm. The lessons learned from their time apart became instrumental in redefining the future of Flosstradamus.

The Future Sound of Flosstradamus

As Flosstradamus set their sights on a new chapter, the impact of their solo projects became evident in their evolving sound. The fusion of genres, incorporation of live elements, and the introduction of diverse collaborations enriched their musical palette. The duo embraced a more eclectic approach, merging trap, hip-hop, and electronic influences into a cohesive sound that resonated with both long-time fans and new listeners.

The future direction of Flosstradamus was thus shaped by the individual journeys of its members. The experiences gained during their time apart not only enhanced their artistry but also solidified their bond as collaborators. The lessons learned from exploring their unique styles, collaborating with various artists, and navigating the complexities of fame ultimately led to a more robust and innovative Flosstradamus.

Conclusion

In conclusion, the impact of solo projects on Flosstradamus' future direction cannot be overstated. The individual artistic explorations of Josh and Curt served as a catalyst for growth, innovation, and reinvention. As they rejoined forces, the duo emerged with a renewed sense of purpose and a richer musical identity. The experiences gained during their solo endeavors laid the groundwork for a future that promises to be as dynamic and exciting as their journey thus far. Flosstradamus stands poised to continue influencing the EDM landscape, armed with the knowledge and creativity garnered from their time apart.

Chapter Four: Reinvention and Resurgence

The Reunion

Reuniting as Flosstradamus: A New Beginning

In the ever-evolving landscape of electronic dance music (EDM), few stories are as compelling as that of Flosstradamus. After a period of personal and creative exploration, the duo, consisting of Josh Young and Curt Cameruci, found themselves at a crossroads. The decision to reunite was not just a nostalgic return to their roots; it was a strategic move toward reinvention and growth. This chapter delves into the dynamics of their reunion, the challenges they faced, and the exhilarating possibilities that lay ahead.

The Catalyst for Reunion

The decision to reunite Flosstradamus came after a series of introspective moments for both members. Each had embarked on solo projects that allowed them to explore their individual artistic identities. Josh, with his forays into various genres, and Curt, who dabbled in rediscovering his passion for music, both realized that while solo endeavors were fulfilling, there was an irreplaceable synergy when they collaborated. This realization was akin to the equation:

$$S_{total} = S_{Josh} + S_{Curt} + S_{collaboration} \tag{28}$$

Where S represents the sound quality and artistic expression of each member and their collaborative efforts. The reunion promised to amplify their combined talents, creating a new sound that was both fresh and familiar.

Reconnecting with Their Fan Base

One of the first steps in their reunion was to reconnect with their fan base. During their hiatus, the EDM scene had transformed significantly, with new trends and artists emerging. Flosstradamus had to navigate this new landscape while rekindling the loyalty of their original fans. The duo initiated this process through social media campaigns, engaging their audience with throwback posts, behind-the-scenes footage, and interactive Q&A sessions. They understood that their fans had grown alongside them, and it was essential to acknowledge this shared journey.

To further solidify this reconnection, Flosstradamus organized a series of intimate pop-up shows. These events were designed to create an exclusive experience for their most dedicated supporters. The response was overwhelming, with tickets selling out in minutes, demonstrating the enduring love for their music. This phenomenon can be expressed through the following relationship:

$$E_{engagement} = f(T_{intimacy}, A_{accessibility}) \tag{29}$$

Where $E_{engagement}$ represents the level of fan engagement, $T_{intimacy}$ refers to the closeness of the events, and $A_{accessibility}$ denotes the ease of access to these experiences. Their strategy proved effective, leading to a resurgence in their popularity.

Redefining Their Sound and Identity

As Flosstradamus re-entered the music scene, they faced the daunting task of redefining their sound and identity. The EDM landscape had shifted, with new sub-genres and production techniques emerging. The duo recognized that they needed to evolve while staying true to their roots. This balancing act required a deep understanding of their musical influences and the current trends in the industry.

They began experimenting with a blend of their classic trap sound infused with elements from other genres, such as hip-hop, rock, and even orchestral music. This innovative approach not only revitalized their music but also attracted a broader audience. The equation governing their sound evolution could be represented as:

$$S_{new} = S_{old} + \Delta S_{influences} \tag{30}$$

Where S_{new} is the new sound, S_{old} is the original sound, and $\Delta S_{influences}$ represents the changes and additions brought in from various musical styles. This formula encapsulated their journey of transformation, allowing them to craft tracks that resonated with both longtime fans and newcomers.

Stepping Into the Future: Flosstradamus 2.0

With their reunion solidified and a fresh sound on the horizon, Flosstradamus was poised to step into the future as a revitalized entity—Flosstradamus 2.0. This new chapter was marked by ambitious projects, including collaborations with emerging artists and the integration of live instrumentation into their performances. The duo recognized the importance of staying relevant in a fast-paced industry and sought to innovate continuously.

Their live shows evolved into immersive experiences, incorporating visual artistry, storytelling, and audience interaction. By blending traditional DJ sets with live performances, they created a unique concert experience that set them apart from their peers. The impact of this transformation can be illustrated by the equation:

$$C_{experience} = I_{innovation} + A_{audience\_interaction} + V_{visuals} \qquad (31)$$

Where $C_{experience}$ represents the overall concert experience, $I_{innovation}$ refers to the creative elements introduced, $A_{audience\_interaction}$ denotes the engagement with the audience, and $V_{visuals}$ encapsulates the visual components of the show. This multifaceted approach ensured that Flosstradamus not only retained their fan base but also attracted a new generation of listeners.

Conclusion: A New Chapter in the Flosstradamus Saga

The reunion of Flosstradamus marked a significant turning point in their careers. It was a testament to their resilience, creativity, and enduring friendship. As they embarked on this new journey, they embraced the challenges and opportunities that lay ahead, determined to leave an indelible mark on the EDM landscape. With their sights set on the future, Flosstradamus was ready to redefine what it meant to be a modern music duo, proving that sometimes, a new beginning is precisely what you need to soar to new heights.

In summary, the reunion of Flosstradamus was not merely a return to the stage; it was a strategic evolution, a rekindling of creative fires, and a celebration of the bond that had originally forged their path in the world of music. As they embraced the future, one thing was clear: the echoes of their past would continue to resonate, shaping their legacy for years to come.

Reconnecting with Their Fan Base

In the world of music, especially within the fast-paced realm of electronic dance music (EDM), maintaining a strong connection with one's fan base can often feel like trying to catch smoke with your bare hands. For Flosstradamus, the journey back to their fans was not merely a strategic business move; it was a heartfelt reconnection with the very essence of what made them who they are.

Understanding the Disconnect

After a period of intense touring and the pressures of mainstream success, Flosstradamus found themselves at a crossroads. The whirlwind of fame often creates a barrier between artists and their fans. As they ascended to new heights, the intimate interactions that once defined their early gigs became overshadowed by larger venues and festival stages. This shift can lead to a sense of alienation, both for the artists and their supporters.

The theory of *social presence* suggests that the sense of connection and engagement between artists and fans is crucial for a sustainable fan relationship. As defined by Short, Williams, and Christie (1976), social presence is the degree to which a person is perceived as "real" in a mediated communication environment. For Flosstradamus, the challenge was to re-establish that sense of reality and intimacy that had been lost.

Engaging Through Social Media

To bridge this gap, Flosstradamus turned to social media platforms. With millions of followers across various channels, they recognized the potential of these platforms to foster a more personal connection. They began sharing behind-the-scenes content, candid moments from their lives, and even snippets of their creative process. This approach, grounded in the principles of *relationship marketing*, allowed them to cultivate a more genuine relationship with their audience.

For instance, during the production of their new album, they initiated a series of live Q&A sessions on Instagram and Twitter. Fans were invited to ask questions, share their thoughts, and even contribute ideas. This not only made fans feel valued but also reinvigorated their interest in Flosstradamus' music. The engagement metrics skyrocketed, with interactions increasing by over 300% during this period.

Creating Exclusive Experiences

Recognizing the power of exclusivity, Flosstradamus also launched a series of intimate events and pop-up shows. These smaller gatherings allowed them to interact directly with their fans, providing an experience that was both personal and memorable. The concept of *experiential marketing* came into play, where fans were not just passive listeners but active participants in the Flosstradamus journey.

An example of this was their "Back to the Roots" tour, where they performed in smaller venues reminiscent of their early days. The setlist included fan-favorite tracks and unreleased material, creating an atmosphere of nostalgia and excitement. The response was overwhelmingly positive, with fans expressing their appreciation for the chance to see their favorite duo in a more intimate setting.

Feedback Loops and Adaptation

Furthermore, Flosstradamus implemented a feedback loop to continuously gauge fan sentiment. Through surveys and direct feedback on social media, they sought to understand what their audience wanted. This adaptive approach is rooted in the concept of *agile marketing*, which emphasizes the importance of being responsive to customer needs and preferences.

For example, after receiving feedback about the desire for more collaborative projects, Flosstradamus began to explore partnerships with emerging artists. This not only revitalized their sound but also introduced their fan base to new talent, further enriching the community around their music.

Conclusion: A Two-Way Street

Ultimately, reconnecting with their fan base was not just about Flosstradamus reaching out; it was about creating a two-way street of communication and engagement. By leveraging social media, offering exclusive experiences, and actively seeking feedback, they were able to rebuild the bridge that had been compromised during their rise to fame.

As they moved forward, Flosstradamus recognized that their fans are not just supporters; they are an integral part of their musical journey. This realization transformed their approach to music and marketing, ensuring that the echoes of their past resonated beautifully in the present and future.

In conclusion, the journey of reconnection was a testament to the enduring power of community in the music industry. Flosstradamus not only found their way back to their roots but also paved the way for a new era of interaction and collaboration, ensuring that their legacy would continue to thrive in the hearts of their fans.

Redefining Their Sound and Identity

In the ever-evolving landscape of electronic dance music (EDM), the journey of Flosstradamus is a testament to the power of reinvention. After a hiatus that allowed both Josh and Curt to explore their individual musical identities, their reunion marked a pivotal moment in redefining not just their sound but their very essence as artists. This metamorphosis was driven by several key factors that influenced their creative direction and identity.

Embracing Change

The EDM scene is notorious for its rapid shifts in trends and styles. As such, Flosstradamus recognized the necessity of evolving their sound to stay relevant. They ventured beyond their established trap roots, which had initially defined their identity, and began experimenting with a fusion of genres. This included elements of pop, hip-hop, and even live instrumentation, which they had previously shied away from.

For instance, their collaboration with artists from different genres allowed them to infuse fresh perspectives into their music. By working with vocalists and musicians, they created a more dynamic sound that resonated with a broader audience. This shift not only revitalized their music but also redefined their identity as versatile producers rather than just DJs.

Theoretical Underpinnings

The concept of identity in music can be analyzed through the lens of *musical semiotics*, which examines how music communicates meaning through signs and symbols. According to theorist Jean-Jacques Nattiez, music is a system of signs that can convey different messages depending on the context in which it is presented. Flosstradamus' reinvention can be seen as a response to the semiotic demands of a changing audience that craved innovation and authenticity.

This concept is further illustrated by the *cultural capital* theory proposed by Pierre Bourdieu, which posits that artists must navigate and negotiate their identities within the cultural marketplace. By adopting a more eclectic sound, Flosstradamus not only broadened their appeal but also elevated their cultural capital, allowing them to maintain relevance in a competitive industry.

Challenges Faced

However, this journey of redefining their sound was not without its challenges. The duo faced internal conflicts as they grappled with their artistic visions. Josh leaned towards a more experimental approach, while Curt preferred to retain some of the classic trap elements that had brought them initial success. This divergence led to creative tensions that required open dialogue and compromise.

Moreover, the pressure to meet fan expectations while simultaneously pushing boundaries created a delicate balancing act. The fear of alienating their core audience loomed large, as they ventured into uncharted musical territory. This challenge is common in the music industry, where artists must often weigh the desire for innovation against the risk of losing their established fan base.

Examples of Reinvention

One notable example of their reinvention can be found in their single, *"Mosh Pit,"* which features a blend of heavy bass lines, energetic beats, and catchy hooks that appeal to both EDM enthusiasts and mainstream listeners. The incorporation of vocal elements and a more melodic structure marked a significant departure from their earlier work, showcasing their growth as artists.

Additionally, their collaboration with prominent figures in the hip-hop community, such as Juicy J and Waka Flocka Flame, exemplified their commitment to crossing genre boundaries. These collaborations not only enriched their sound but also positioned them as key players in the broader musical dialogue, further solidifying their identity as innovators.

Conclusion

In conclusion, the process of redefining their sound and identity was a multifaceted journey for Flosstradamus. By embracing change, navigating challenges, and drawing on theoretical frameworks, they successfully transformed their musical output while maintaining their core essence. This evolution not only revitalized their career but also reaffirmed their status as influential figures in the EDM landscape, paving the way for future generations of artists to explore the limitless possibilities of sound.

Stepping Into the Future: Flosstradamus 2.0

As the curtain rose on the next chapter of Flosstradamus, the duo found themselves at a crossroads, balancing the nostalgia of their past with the excitement of potential futures. This rebirth, dubbed Flosstradamus 2.0, was not merely a rebranding; it was a profound transformation that sought to redefine their identity in a rapidly evolving musical landscape.

Embracing Change

The first step in this evolution was acknowledging the changing dynamics of the EDM scene. With the rise of new genres and the influx of fresh talent, Flosstradamus recognized the necessity to adapt. The challenge lay in maintaining the essence of their sound while incorporating innovative elements that resonated with both old fans and a new generation. This balancing act can be mathematically represented as follows:

$$S_{new} = S_{old} + \Delta S \tag{32}$$

Where: - S_{new} is the new sound, - S_{old} is the original sound, - ΔS represents the changes and innovations introduced.

This equation highlights that the essence of Flosstradamus remains intact while allowing for growth and adaptation.

Reconnecting with Their Fan Base

Reconnecting with their fan base was crucial for Flosstradamus 2.0. The duo employed a strategy that involved engaging fans through social media, live Q&A sessions, and exclusive behind-the-scenes content. This direct interaction not only rekindled old relationships but also fostered a sense of community. They implemented fan feedback into their creative process, leading to a more inclusive and collaborative atmosphere.

For instance, the duo launched a campaign titled "Your Sound, Our Beats," inviting fans to submit sound samples for potential use in their new tracks. This initiative not only generated excitement but also reinforced the bond between the artists and their audience, demonstrating a shift from a traditional artist-fan relationship to a more collaborative partnership.

Redefining Their Sound and Identity

With the groundwork laid, Flosstradamus embarked on the ambitious task of redefining their sound. They experimented with live instruments, integrating guitar riffs and brass sections into their tracks, creating a hybrid sound that blurred the lines between electronic and live music. This fusion can be mathematically represented as:

$$M = \sum_{i=1}^{n}(E_i + L_i) \tag{33}$$

Where: - M is the new musical composition, - E_i represents the electronic elements, - L_i denotes the live instruments, - n is the number of distinct elements in the composition.

This formula illustrates how the duo meticulously crafted a sound that was both familiar and refreshingly new.

Stepping Into the Future: The Vision

The vision for Flosstradamus 2.0 extended beyond mere sound. The duo sought to enhance the live experience, transforming concerts into immersive events. They incorporated cutting-edge technology, such as augmented reality (AR) and advanced visual effects, creating a multisensory experience that captivated audiences. The integration of technology into live performances can be analyzed through the following framework:

$$E_{experience} = T + V + A \tag{34}$$

Where: - $E_{experience}$ is the overall concert experience, - T represents the technology used, - V denotes the visual elements, - A signifies the auditory components.

This equation underscores the importance of a holistic approach to live performances, where each component contributes to an unforgettable experience.

Collaborations and Innovations

Flosstradamus 2.0 also embraced collaborations with a diverse array of artists, pushing the boundaries of their musical palette. They worked with genre-defying musicians, fusing trap with elements of rock, jazz, and even classical music. This collaborative spirit not only enriched their sound but also showcased their versatility as producers and artists.

For example, their collaboration with a renowned jazz trumpeter resulted in a track that seamlessly blended trap beats with soulful brass melodies, exemplifying their commitment to innovation. This collaborative model can be represented as:

$$C_{total} = \sum_{j=1}^{m} C_j \qquad (35)$$

Where: - C_{total} is the total collaborative output, - C_j represents each unique collaboration, - m is the number of collaborations.

This equation illustrates how each partnership added a unique layer to their evolving sound.

Conclusion: A New Dawn

In conclusion, Flosstradamus 2.0 marked a significant evolution in the duo's journey. By embracing change, reconnecting with their fan base, redefining their sound, and innovating their live performances, they not only stepped into the future but also laid the groundwork for a lasting legacy. As they continue to push boundaries and explore new horizons, the echoes of their past resonate harmoniously with the promises of tomorrow. The journey of Flosstradamus is far from over; in fact, it has only just begun.

Collaborations and Innovations

Joining Forces with Other Artists

Collaboration in the music industry is akin to a culinary fusion where diverse ingredients combine to create a dish that tantalizes the senses. For Flosstradamus, joining forces with other artists not only expanded their sonic palette but also solidified their position as innovators in the EDM landscape. This section delves into the significance, challenges, and outcomes of these collaborations, showcasing how Flosstradamus transformed their sound through partnerships.

The Significance of Collaboration

In the world of music, collaboration can lead to a symbiotic relationship where artists share ideas, techniques, and inspirations. As *Bennett (2017)* posits, "Collaboration breeds creativity," and this notion holds particularly true for Flosstradamus. By working with a diverse array of artists, they were able to integrate varying musical styles into their work, pushing the boundaries of their sound.

For instance, their collaboration with the rapper *Waka Flocka Flame* on the track *"No Hands"* introduced an energetic hip-hop influence into their trap-heavy repertoire. This blending of genres not only appealed to a broader audience but also showcased their versatility as producers. The equation governing the collaborative synergy can be expressed as:

$$C = A + B$$

where C represents the collaborative output, and A and B are the individual contributions of each artist. The result, C, is often greater than the sum of its parts, leading to innovation and creativity that neither artist could achieve alone.

Challenges in Collaboration

However, collaboration is not without its challenges. Differing artistic visions, creative egos, and logistical constraints can complicate the process. As noted by *Smith (2019)*, "Navigating the waters of collaboration requires patience, understanding, and sometimes, a bit of compromise."

For Flosstradamus, one notable challenge arose during their work with the electronic duo *Tchami*. While both parties shared a passion for electronic music, their distinct approaches to production created tension. Tchami's deep house influence contrasted with Flosstradamus' trap roots, leading to discussions that required careful negotiation. This scenario illustrates the importance of effective communication and mutual respect in collaborative endeavors, echoing the sentiment that:

$$E = \frac{P}{R}$$

where E is the effectiveness of the collaboration, P is the productive output, and R is the resistance faced during the creative process. A lower resistance, achieved through open dialogue, often leads to a higher effectiveness.

Notable Collaborations and Their Impact

The partnership with *Dillon Francis* on the track *"Get Low"* serves as a prime example of successful collaboration. This track not only became a festival anthem but also marked a significant moment in the trap genre's evolution. The infectious beat, combined with Francis' distinctive sound design, resulted in a track that resonated with audiences worldwide.

Moreover, their collaboration with *Baauer* on the remix of *"Harlem Shake"* further solidified their reputation as trendsetters. This remix, which incorporated elements of trap and bass music, showcased their ability to adapt and innovate within the rapidly changing EDM landscape. The success of these collaborations can be quantified through streaming metrics, illustrating the growing demand for genre-blending tracks:

$$S = \frac{T}{C}$$

where S represents the streaming success, T is the total streams, and C is the number of collaborations. As the number of collaborations increases, so too does the potential for viral success.

Conclusion

In conclusion, joining forces with other artists has been pivotal for Flosstradamus in their journey of reinvention and resurgence. Through collaboration, they have not only expanded their musical horizons but also contributed to the evolution of the EDM genre. While challenges exist in the collaborative process, the rewards often outweigh the difficulties, leading to innovative sounds that resonate with fans and influence future artists. As they continue to explore new partnerships, Flosstradamus remains a testament to the power of collaboration in the ever-evolving landscape of music.

Expanding Their Musical Arsenal: Live Instruments and Vocals

As Flosstradamus embarked on their journey of reinvention, they discovered the transformative power of integrating live instruments and vocals into their performances. This marked a pivotal shift in their musical identity, one that not only enhanced their sound but also deepened their connection with audiences.

The decision to incorporate live elements stemmed from a desire to create a more immersive experience for fans. By blending the electronic with the organic, Flosstradamus aimed to break down the barriers often associated with DJ performances. The idea was simple yet profound: why not bring the energy of a live band into the realm of electronic music?

Theoretical Framework

From a theoretical standpoint, the integration of live instruments into electronic music can be understood through the lens of hybridization. Hybridization, in music, refers to the blending of different genres, styles, or performance techniques to create something new and innovative. This concept is well-documented in music theory, particularly in the analysis of cross-genre influences and the evolution of musical forms. The equation that represents this hybridization can be simplified as follows:

$$H = E + L$$

where H represents the hybrid sound, E denotes electronic elements, and L signifies live instrumentation. The successful fusion of these components relies heavily on the careful balance of each element, ensuring that neither overshadows the other.

Challenges Encountered

However, this ambitious endeavor was not without its challenges. One of the primary issues Flosstradamus faced was the logistical complexity of incorporating live musicians into their performances. This required not only a reconfiguration of their stage setup but also a significant investment in rehearsal time and coordination. The band had to ensure that the live musicians were well-versed in their tracks, which often involved intricate arrangements and rapid tempo changes.

Moreover, the introduction of live vocals presented its own set of hurdles. Finding the right vocalists who could seamlessly blend with their established sound was crucial. The band experimented with various artists, each bringing their unique flair, but it took time to find the perfect match. Additionally, the unpredictability of live performances—such as equipment malfunctions or vocal missteps—added an element of risk that was less prevalent in their previous DJ sets.

Examples of Integration

Despite these challenges, the results were nothing short of exhilarating. One of the standout moments in their evolution came during a performance at the Electric Daisy Carnival, where they collaborated with a live drummer and a saxophonist. The synergy between the electronic beats and the organic rhythms created an electrifying atmosphere that resonated with the audience.

The incorporation of live instruments also allowed for spontaneous improvisation, which became a hallmark of their shows. For instance, during a remix of their hit track "Rollup," the saxophonist took center stage, weaving melodic lines that complemented the driving bass drops. This not only showcased the musicianship of the performers but also elevated the overall energy of the performance.

The Impact on Their Sound

The integration of live instruments and vocals fundamentally altered Flosstradamus' sound. Their tracks began to feature richer textures and dynamic layers that were previously absent. For example, the addition of live strings in their remix of "Cannonball" introduced a lushness that transformed the track into a euphoric anthem, captivating fans both old and new.

Furthermore, this evolution had a ripple effect on their songwriting process. With live musicians involved, the creative possibilities expanded exponentially. The band found themselves experimenting with different time signatures, chord progressions, and arrangements, leading to a more diverse catalog of music. The collaborative spirit fostered by these live sessions encouraged innovation, pushing the boundaries of what Flosstradamus could achieve.

Conclusion

In conclusion, the decision to expand their musical arsenal by incorporating live instruments and vocals was a defining moment for Flosstradamus. It not only enriched their sound but also redefined their identity as artists. By embracing the hybridization of electronic and live music, they created a unique experience that resonated deeply with fans. This evolution not only showcased their adaptability but also solidified their place as pioneers in the ever-evolving landscape of electronic dance music.

As they continue to push the envelope, Flosstradamus stands as a testament to the power of innovation in music, proving that the echoes of their past can harmonize beautifully with the symphonies of the future.

Pushing Boundaries: Fusing Genres and Styles

In the ever-evolving landscape of electronic dance music (EDM), Flosstradamus has consistently pushed the boundaries of musical genres and styles, creating a unique sonic identity that resonates with fans across the globe. The duo's innovative approach to music production has not only redefined their sound but has also set a precedent for other artists in the industry. This section delves into the theoretical underpinnings of genre fusion, the challenges faced during this creative process, and notable examples of Flosstradamus' genre-blending masterpieces.

Theoretical Framework: Understanding Genre Fusion

At its core, genre fusion involves the integration of elements from different musical styles to create a new, hybrid sound. Theoretical frameworks such as *Intertextuality* and *Cultural Appropriation* provide insight into how artists can draw from various genres while navigating the complexities of musical identity.

Intertextuality, as defined by literary theorist Julia Kristeva, suggests that all texts (or in this case, musical works) are interconnected and influenced by one another. This means that when Flosstradamus incorporates elements from hip-hop, trap, and electronic music, they are engaging in a dialogue with these genres, acknowledging their influences while simultaneously creating something new. The equation that can represent this relationship is:

$$\text{New Genre} = f(\text{Genre A}, \text{Genre B}, \text{Genre C}) \qquad (36)$$

Where f is a function that denotes the fusion process, and Genre A, Genre B, Genre C are the different musical styles being combined.

However, the act of fusing genres is not without its challenges. Issues such as *authenticity* and *cultural sensitivity* often arise. Artists must be mindful of how they represent the genres they draw from, ensuring that they do not exploit or misrepresent the cultural significance of those styles. This requires a delicate balance of respect and innovation, which Flosstradamus navigates with finesse.

Challenges in Genre Fusion

Despite their success, Flosstradamus has faced several challenges while pushing the boundaries of genre fusion. One significant issue is the risk of alienating their core fan base, which may have specific expectations regarding the duo's sound. As they experimented with incorporating live instruments and diverse musical elements, some fans expressed concern that their original sound was becoming diluted.

Moreover, the technical challenges of blending genres can be daunting. Each genre has its own conventions, structures, and production techniques. For example, the syncopated rhythms of trap music differ significantly from the four-on-the-floor beats typical in house music. Successfully merging these elements requires a deep understanding of music theory and production techniques, as well as a willingness to experiment and take risks.

Notable Examples of Genre Fusion

Flosstradamus has produced several tracks that exemplify their genre-blending prowess. One standout example is their collaboration with the rapper *Lil Jon* on the track *"Turn Down for What"*. This song seamlessly melds trap beats with hip-hop elements, creating an anthem that dominated dance floors and radio waves alike. The infectious energy and catchy hooks exemplify how Flosstradamus effectively fuses genres to create music that is both innovative and accessible.

Another notable example is their remix of *"Roll Up"* by *Wiz Khalifa*. In this remix, Flosstradamus incorporates elements of dubstep, layering heavy bass drops with Khalifa's laid-back flow. This fusion not only showcases their ability to reinterpret existing tracks but also highlights their talent for creating a sound that appeals to fans of both hip-hop and EDM.

Furthermore, their track *"Mosh Pit"* features an eclectic mix of electronic sounds, trap beats, and even hints of rock influences. The dynamic shifts in tempo and energy throughout the song exemplify the duo's commitment to pushing musical boundaries and experimenting with different styles.

Conclusion

Through their fearless exploration of genre fusion, Flosstradamus has established themselves as pioneers in the EDM scene. Their ability to blend diverse musical styles not only enriches their own sound but also contributes to the broader evolution of electronic music. As they continue to innovate and challenge the status quo, Flosstradamus remains a testament to the power of creativity and collaboration in the music industry. Their journey serves as an inspiration for aspiring artists to embrace the beauty of genre fusion and to push the boundaries of their own musical identities.

The Rise of Flosstradamus as Producers and Industry Leaders

As Flosstradamus evolved from a dynamic DJ duo into influential producers and industry leaders, they navigated the complexities of the modern music landscape with the agility of a cat on a hot tin roof—if that cat were also a master of trap beats and had a knack for innovative collaborations. The rise of Flosstradamus in this new role can be attributed to several key factors, including their unique approach to production, strategic partnerships, and their ability to adapt to the ever-changing demands of the music industry.

Innovative Production Techniques

Flosstradamus distinguished themselves through innovative production techniques that broke the mold of traditional EDM. They embraced a hybrid model that combined digital production with live instrumentation, allowing them to create rich, textured soundscapes that resonated with audiences. This approach can be expressed mathematically as:

$$S = \sum_{i=1}^{n}(a_i \cdot b_i)$$

where S represents the overall sound quality, a_i are the digital elements, and b_i are the live instruments. The synergy between these two components not only enhanced their tracks but also set a new standard in the EDM genre.

Collaborative Endeavors

The duo's ability to collaborate with a diverse range of artists further solidified their status as industry leaders. By working with established names and emerging talents alike, Flosstradamus expanded their musical repertoire and introduced fresh perspectives into their work. Notable collaborations include their remix of "*Get Low*" by Dillon Francis and DJ Snake, which became a cultural phenomenon and showcased their ability to blend genres seamlessly.

This collaborative spirit can be likened to the concept of *synergy*, where the whole becomes greater than the sum of its parts. For instance, in a mathematical representation:

$$Synergy = A + B + C > A + B + C$$

where A, B, and C are individual contributions from each artist. This principle not only applied to their music but also to their brand, as they began to influence trends and styles across the EDM landscape.

Navigating Industry Challenges

Despite their success, Flosstradamus faced numerous challenges as they transitioned into their roles as producers. The music industry is notorious for its rapid pace and shifting dynamics, often leaving artists scrambling to keep up. Issues such as copyright disputes, evolving listener preferences, and the impact of streaming services posed significant hurdles.

One notable challenge was the rise of digital distribution platforms, which altered how music was consumed and monetized. Flosstradamus had to adapt their marketing strategies and embrace new technologies to maintain relevance. This adaptability can be modeled by the equation:

$$R = f(T, C)$$

where R represents relevance, T is the adoption of technology, and C is the ability to connect with contemporary culture. By effectively managing these variables, they ensured their continued success in a competitive environment.

Establishing a Lasting Impact

As producers, Flosstradamus not only shaped their own sound but also influenced the broader EDM community. They became trendsetters, introducing new styles and techniques that inspired a wave of upcoming artists. Their production work extended beyond their own releases, as they took on roles as mentors and collaborators, helping to cultivate the next generation of musicians.

An example of this mentorship is their involvement in various music festivals and workshops, where they shared their knowledge of production techniques and industry insights. This commitment to fostering new talent reflects their understanding of the importance of legacy in the music industry, which can be encapsulated in the formula:

$$L = \sum_{j=1}^{m} T_j$$

where L is the legacy, and T_j represents the contributions of each artist they mentored. Through these efforts, Flosstradamus solidified their position not just as producers, but as pivotal figures in the evolution of EDM.

In conclusion, the rise of Flosstradamus as producers and industry leaders is a testament to their innovative spirit, collaborative nature, and resilience in the face of challenges. They have not only redefined their own sound but have also left an indelible mark on the EDM landscape, ensuring that their influence will be felt for years to come. As they continue to push boundaries and explore new horizons, one can only imagine what echoes they will leave behind in the ever-evolving world of music.

Dealing with Expectations and Criticism

As Flosstradamus embarked on their journey into the limelight, they quickly discovered that with great success comes an avalanche of expectations and criticism. This phenomenon is not unique to the duo; it is a common thread woven through the fabric of the music industry. The pressure to continuously innovate while pleasing a diverse fan base can feel like trying to juggle flaming swords while riding a unicycle on a tightrope strung over a pit of snapping alligators.

The Weight of Expectation

The expectations placed upon artists can often be quantified through a concept known as the *Expectation-Performance Gap* (EPG). The EPG is defined as:

$$EPG = E - P \qquad (37)$$

where E represents the expectations of fans and critics, and P signifies the actual performance or output of the artist. For Flosstradamus, the gap began to widen as their early mixtapes garnered immense popularity. Fans expected the duo to consistently deliver groundbreaking tracks that would redefine the EDM genre. However, the reality of artistic creation is that it is often a nonlinear process, filled with ebbs and flows.

Navigating Criticism

Criticism, especially in the age of social media, can manifest in various forms—ranging from constructive feedback to outright vitriol. The duo faced scrutiny not only from fans but also from industry insiders who questioned their artistic choices. One notable instance occurred after the release of their experimental track *"Bass Drop Apocalypse."* While some hailed it as a bold evolution of their sound, others criticized it as a departure from their roots. This duality of reception illustrates the *Cognitive Dissonance Theory*, which posits that individuals experience discomfort when confronted with conflicting beliefs or ideas.

This dissonance can lead to a phenomenon known as *Backlash*, where fans who feel betrayed by an artist's new direction may vocalize their dissatisfaction. For Flosstradamus, the backlash was palpable, leading to a period of introspection. The duo had to ask themselves: *How do we stay true to our artistic vision while also honoring the expectations of our fan base?*

Strategies for Coping

To navigate this treacherous terrain, Flosstradamus employed several strategies:

1. **Open Communication:** They began engaging with their fans through social media platforms, sharing their creative process and the motivations behind their musical choices. By demystifying their work, they fostered a sense of community and understanding.

2. **Embracing Constructive Criticism:** Rather than shying away from feedback, they actively sought out constructive criticism. This approach allowed them to refine their sound while remaining receptive to their audience's desires.

3. **Prioritizing Artistic Integrity:** Ultimately, Flosstradamus recognized that their primary responsibility was to their art. They made a conscious decision to prioritize their creative instincts over external pressures, leading to a more authentic and fulfilling musical output.

The Impact of Expectations on Creativity

The interplay between expectations and creativity can be complex. Research in the field of *Psychology of Creativity* suggests that excessive pressure can stifle innovation. A study conducted by [?] found that when individuals perceive their work as being evaluated, their intrinsic motivation diminishes, leading to less creative outcomes. For Flosstradamus, this meant finding a delicate balance between meeting expectations and nurturing their creative impulses.

Conclusion

In conclusion, dealing with expectations and criticism is an inevitable part of the artistic journey, especially for a duo as influential as Flosstradamus. By embracing open communication, valuing constructive feedback, and prioritizing their artistic integrity, they have not only managed to navigate the turbulent waters of public perception but have also emerged stronger and more resilient. In the end, it is this resilience that will continue to shape their legacy in the ever-evolving landscape of electronic music.

Chapter Five: A Legacy in Motion

Influencing the Next Generation

Mentoring Upcoming Artists

In the ever-evolving landscape of electronic dance music (EDM), the importance of mentorship cannot be overstated. For Flosstradamus, the journey from local heroes to global icons has equipped them with invaluable insights and experiences, which they are now eager to share with the next generation of musicians. This section explores their mentoring efforts, highlighting the challenges, theories, and examples that shape their approach.

The Importance of Mentorship in Music

Mentorship in music serves as a bridge for aspiring artists, connecting them to industry knowledge, practical skills, and emotional support. According to [?], effective mentorship can significantly enhance an artist's development by providing guidance on both creative and business aspects. This duality is especially crucial in the fast-paced world of EDM, where trends shift rapidly, and innovation is key to standing out.

Challenges Faced by Upcoming Artists

While the EDM scene is vibrant and full of opportunities, it also presents several challenges for emerging artists. These include:

- **Navigating the Industry:** Many new artists struggle to understand the complex dynamics of the music industry, from contract negotiations to branding.

+ **Maintaining Authenticity:** With the pressure to conform to popular trends, upcoming artists often grapple with staying true to their unique sound.

+ **Building a Fanbase:** In an oversaturated market, establishing a loyal following can be daunting, requiring strategic marketing and engagement.

Flosstradamus recognizes these challenges and aims to provide a supportive environment where upcoming artists can thrive.

The Mentoring Approach of Flosstradamus

Flosstradamus employs a multi-faceted approach to mentoring, which includes:

1. **Workshops and Masterclasses:** They frequently host workshops where they share their expertise in production techniques, live performance strategies, and the business of music. These sessions are designed to demystify the creative process and provide actionable insights.

2. **Collaborative Projects:** By inviting emerging artists to collaborate on tracks, Flosstradamus fosters a hands-on learning experience. This collaboration not only enhances the skills of the mentees but also allows them to gain exposure through Flosstradamus' established platforms.

3. **Networking Opportunities:** Understanding the significance of connections, Flosstradamus actively introduces upcoming artists to industry professionals, helping them build relationships that can lead to future collaborations and gigs.

Case Studies

To illustrate the effectiveness of their mentoring approach, consider the following examples:

+ **Artist A:** An up-and-coming DJ who struggled with production techniques attended a Flosstradamus workshop. With guidance on software and sound design, Artist A was able to produce their first EP, which gained traction on streaming platforms, leading to several festival bookings.

+ **Artist B:** A producer known for their unique sound was brought in for a collaborative project with Flosstradamus. This partnership not only elevated Artist B's profile but also resulted in a hit track that topped EDM charts, showcasing the power of collaboration in the mentoring process.

Theoretical Framework

The mentoring practices of Flosstradamus can be analyzed through the lens of social learning theory, which posits that individuals learn from observing and interacting with others [?]. This theory emphasizes the role of role models in shaping behavior and skills. By serving as mentors, Flosstradamus not only imparts knowledge but also inspires upcoming artists to emulate their work ethic, creativity, and resilience.

Conclusion

In conclusion, Flosstradamus' commitment to mentoring upcoming artists is a testament to their understanding of the music industry's intricacies. By providing guidance, resources, and opportunities, they are not just shaping the future of EDM but also ensuring that their legacy continues through the success of those they mentor. As they look to the future, Flosstradamus remains dedicated to nurturing the next generation of talent, ensuring that the echoes of their influence resonate for years to come.

The Flosstradamus Sound in Contemporary Music

The sound of Flosstradamus has not only carved a niche in the EDM landscape but has also significantly influenced contemporary music across various genres. Their unique blend of trap, hip-hop, and electronic elements has become a defining characteristic that resonates with both fans and fellow artists alike. This section explores the impact of the Flosstradamus sound on contemporary music, delving into its theoretical underpinnings, notable problems, and concrete examples.

Theoretical Foundations

At the core of Flosstradamus' sound lies the fusion of trap beats with electronic music. Trap, characterized by its use of hi-hats, heavy bass, and syncopated rhythms, provides a rhythmic foundation that is both infectious and danceable. The incorporation of electronic elements—such as synths, samples, and digital effects—adds layers of complexity and texture to their tracks.

Mathematically, the rhythm can be analyzed using the following equation:

$$R(t) = A \cdot \sin(\omega t + \phi) \tag{38}$$

Where: - $R(t)$ represents the rhythm at time t, - A is the amplitude (volume), - ω is the angular frequency (determining the tempo), - ϕ is the phase shift (which can create variations in the beat).

This equation illustrates how the interplay of various elements can create a dynamic soundscape that evolves over time, keeping listeners engaged and energized.

Problems and Challenges

Despite their success, Flosstradamus has faced challenges in maintaining their sound's relevance amid the rapidly evolving music scene. One significant issue is the saturation of the trap genre. As more artists adopt trap elements, distinguishing their sound becomes increasingly difficult. This has led to a phenomenon known as "genre fatigue," where listeners may become desensitized to the same sonic characteristics.

Moreover, the rise of streaming platforms has altered the way music is consumed, leading to shorter attention spans. To combat this, Flosstradamus has experimented with track lengths and structures, often opting for more concise, impactful compositions that deliver their signature sound without overstaying their welcome.

Examples of Influence

Flosstradamus' influence can be observed in several contemporary artists who have adopted or adapted their sound. For instance, the rise of artists like RL Grime and Baauer can be traced back to the groundwork laid by Flosstradamus. RL Grime's track "Core" features the same heavy bass and intricate rhythms that Flosstradamus popularized, while Baauer's "Harlem Shake" showcases the trap elements that have become synonymous with their style.

In addition to individual artists, Flosstradamus' sound has permeated mainstream pop music. Collaborations with pop artists have resulted in tracks that blend catchy melodies with trap beats, such as their work with the likes of A-Trak and Waka Flocka Flame. These collaborations demonstrate how Flosstradamus has successfully bridged the gap between electronic music and mainstream pop, influencing a broader audience.

Conclusion

The Flosstradamus sound represents a significant evolution in contemporary music, characterized by its innovative fusion of genres and relentless experimentation. As they continue to push boundaries and redefine their sound, their influence remains evident in the works of emerging artists and established musicians alike. The legacy of Flosstradamus is not just in their tracks but in the way they have shaped the sonic landscape of modern music, paving the way for future generations of creators to explore and expand upon their groundbreaking sound.

In summary, the Flosstradamus sound is a vibrant tapestry woven from the threads of trap, hip-hop, and electronic music, demonstrating the power of innovation in the ever-changing world of contemporary music.

Continuing the Legacy: Flosstradamus' Protégés

As Flosstradamus navigated the ever-evolving landscape of electronic dance music (EDM), they recognized the importance of nurturing the next generation of artists. The duo's commitment to mentoring and supporting emerging talent has become a cornerstone of their legacy, ensuring that their influence extends far beyond their own discography. This section explores the various ways in which Flosstradamus has contributed to the careers of their protégés, the challenges faced in this mentorship role, and the broader implications for the EDM community.

Mentorship Programs and Collaborations

Flosstradamus has actively engaged in mentorship through structured programs and informal collaborations. By hosting workshops and masterclasses, they have provided budding artists with insights into the intricacies of music production, branding, and performance. One notable example is their initiative, *Flossy School*, where they invited aspiring producers to learn directly from them in an immersive environment.

The key principles guiding these mentorship efforts include:

+ **Knowledge Transfer:** Sharing technical skills and industry know-how.

+ **Networking Opportunities:** Connecting protégés with industry professionals and potential collaborators.

+ **Creative Freedom:** Encouraging unique artistic expression while providing constructive feedback.

Challenges in Mentorship

While the intention to foster new talent is noble, the process is fraught with challenges. For instance, the pressure to maintain their own brand while promoting others can lead to conflicts of interest. Additionally, the rapidly changing EDM scene means that what worked for Flosstradamus may not necessarily resonate with newer artists.

One significant problem is the potential for *imposter syndrome* among protégés. As they step into the spotlight, many emerging artists grapple with self-doubt, questioning their worthiness in comparison to established names. Flosstradamus has addressed this issue by emphasizing the importance of personal growth over competition, creating a supportive environment where mistakes are viewed as learning opportunities.

Case Studies of Successful Protégés

Several artists have emerged under the guidance of Flosstradamus, each carving out their own niche while embodying aspects of the duo's sonic ethos.

+ **Dillon Francis:** Initially mentored by Flosstradamus, Dillon's unique blend of moombahton and trap drew significant attention. His collaboration with the duo on the track *"Get Low"* is a prime example of how mentorship can lead to successful partnerships.

+ **NGHTMRE:** Known for his high-energy performances and genre-blending tracks, NGHTMRE cites Flosstradamus as a major influence. Their collaborative efforts on remixes have not only elevated NGHTMRE's profile but have also reinforced Flosstradamus' commitment to fostering new talent.

+ **What So Not:** Originally part of the duo *Flume*, What So Not has evolved into a solo artist with a distinct sound. Flosstradamus played a pivotal role in introducing him to a broader audience through festival appearances and joint projects, demonstrating the power of collaboration in mentorship.

The Flosstradamus Sound in Contemporary Music

The influence of Flosstradamus extends beyond individual artists; their sound has permeated contemporary EDM. The signature blend of trap, bass, and hip-hop elements has inspired a wave of new producers who incorporate these styles into their own work.

To quantify this impact, we can analyze the following equation representing the influence of Flosstradamus on the EDM genre:

$$I = \sum_{n=1}^{N} (C_n \cdot E_n) \tag{39}$$

Where:

+ I is the overall influence on the EDM genre.

+ C_n represents the contributions of each protégé n.

+ E_n denotes the engagement and popularity of their music within the community.

+ N is the total number of protégés.

This equation illustrates how the legacy of Flosstradamus is not just a linear progression but a multifaceted influence that continues to evolve as new artists emerge.

Continuing the Legacy

In conclusion, Flosstradamus' dedication to mentoring and supporting their protégés is a testament to their commitment to the future of EDM. By fostering new talent, they ensure that their legacy endures, creating a ripple effect that influences the sound and direction of the genre for years to come. As they continue to collaborate with and uplift emerging artists, Flosstradamus remains a pivotal force in shaping the next generation of musical innovators, proving that the echoes of their impact will resonate long into the future.

Shaping the EDM Industry

Entrepreneurial Ventures and Business Expansions

The journey of Flosstradamus transcends the mere act of creating music; it embodies a robust entrepreneurial spirit that has led to various ventures and business expansions. As the duo evolved from underground artists to mainstream icons, they recognized the importance of diversifying their portfolio, much like a savvy investor who spreads their assets across various sectors to mitigate risk and maximize returns.

Understanding the Entrepreneurial Landscape

In the music industry, entrepreneurial ventures can take many forms, including merchandise sales, brand partnerships, and even launching record labels. For Flosstradamus, the transition from artists to entrepreneurs involved a strategic understanding of market dynamics and consumer behavior. The duo leveraged their growing popularity to explore business opportunities that aligned with their brand identity.

Merchandising: A Profitable Avenue

One of the first entrepreneurial ventures Flosstradamus undertook was the creation of a unique merchandise line. Merchandise in the music industry serves not only as a revenue stream but also as a means of brand reinforcement. The duo's approach was to design apparel that resonated with their fans, incorporating vibrant graphics and slogans that reflected their energetic sound.

The equation for revenue from merchandise can be simplified as:

$$R = P \times Q \tag{40}$$

where:

+ R = total revenue from merchandise

+ P = price per item

+ Q = quantity sold

By hosting pop-up shops at events and collaborating with fashion designers, Flosstradamus successfully turned their merchandise into a desirable product, resulting in significant profit margins.

Brand Partnerships and Collaborations

Recognizing the power of collaboration, Flosstradamus also sought partnerships with brands that aligned with their image. For instance, they partnered with energy drink companies, leveraging their high-energy performances to create synergistic marketing campaigns. These partnerships not only provided financial support but also expanded their reach to new audiences.

The effectiveness of such partnerships can be evaluated through the following relationship:

$$E = \frac{P_A + P_B}{C} \tag{41}$$

where:

+ E = effectiveness of the partnership

- P_A = promotional reach of Flosstradamus

- P_B = promotional reach of the partner brand

- C = cost of collaboration

The result is a win-win scenario where both parties benefit from increased visibility and sales, solidifying Flosstradamus' status as influential brand ambassadors in the music scene.

Launching a Record Label

In a bold move to assert their influence within the industry, Flosstradamus launched their own record label, a venture that allowed them to sign emerging artists and produce music that aligned with their vision. This not only provided a platform for new talent but also positioned Flosstradamus as industry leaders, capable of shaping the future of electronic music.

The operational model of a record label can be expressed as:

$$P = R - C \tag{42}$$

where:

- P = profit from the record label

- R = revenue from music sales and streaming

- C = costs associated with production, marketing, and distribution

By carefully managing costs and focusing on innovative marketing strategies, Flosstradamus maximized their profits while nurturing the next generation of artists.

Innovations in Live Experiences

Flosstradamus also recognized the importance of enhancing the live concert experience. By integrating technology and interactive elements into their performances, they created a unique atmosphere that captivated audiences. This innovation not only set them apart from other acts but also opened new avenues for revenue through ticket sales and sponsorships.

The revenue model for live performances can be illustrated as:

$$T = (N \times P_T) + S \tag{43}$$

where:

+ T = total revenue from live performances

+ N = number of tickets sold

+ P_T = price per ticket

+ S = sponsorship revenue

Through their commitment to innovation, Flosstradamus enhanced their brand value and solidified their position as trendsetters within the EDM landscape.

Conclusion: A Multifaceted Legacy

Flosstradamus' entrepreneurial ventures reflect a keen understanding of the music industry and an ability to adapt to changing market conditions. By diversifying their revenue streams and embracing innovation, they have not only achieved financial success but also left a lasting impact on the music world. Their story serves as a testament to the power of creativity and business acumen, inspiring future generations of artists to pursue their dreams with both passion and strategy.

Flosstradamus as Trendsetters and Taste Makers

In the evolving landscape of electronic dance music (EDM), Flosstradamus has carved out a niche that not only reflects their unique sound but also sets trends that influence the genre as a whole. The duo's ability to blend various musical elements and styles has positioned them as both trendsetters and taste makers within the industry. This section explores their innovative contributions, the challenges they faced, and the examples that illustrate their pivotal role in shaping contemporary music.

Defining the Trendsetting Role

To understand Flosstradamus' impact, we must first define what it means to be a trendsetter and taste maker in the music industry. According to cultural theorist [?], a trendsetter is an individual or group that initiates new styles or movements within a cultural context, while a taste maker is someone who influences the preferences of others. This dual role is essential in the fast-paced world of EDM, where new sounds and styles can emerge overnight.

Innovative Sound and Style

Flosstradamus' sound is characterized by its energetic beats, heavy basslines, and seamless integration of hip-hop elements, particularly in their pioneering work within the trap genre. Their 2013 mixtape, *Soundclash*, serves as a prime example of their innovative approach. The mixtape showcases their ability to blend various genres, creating a unique sound that resonates with a diverse audience.

The equation that encapsulates their sound evolution can be expressed as:

$$S = f(H, E, T) \tag{44}$$

where S represents the Flosstradamus sound, H is hip-hop influences, E is electronic elements, and T is trap music. This formula illustrates how their sound is a function of multiple genres, allowing them to stay ahead of the curve.

Challenges in Trendsetting

While the role of trendsetter comes with opportunities, it also presents significant challenges. One of the primary issues Flosstradamus faced was the risk of being pigeonholed into a single genre. As trap music gained popularity, the duo had to navigate the delicate balance between maintaining their core identity and experimenting with new sounds.

In 2016, they released the track *Came Up*, which incorporated elements of future bass, a genre that was rapidly gaining traction. The decision to explore this new sound was not without its critics, as some fans expressed concern that they were straying too far from their roots. However, this move ultimately solidified their status as innovators, demonstrating their ability to adapt and redefine their sound.

Collaborations and Influences

Flosstradamus' collaborations with other artists have further cemented their role as taste makers. Their partnership with artists like [?], known for his viral hit *Harlem Shake*, resulted in tracks that pushed the boundaries of EDM. The remix of *Harlem Shake* not only showcased their skill in reinterpreting existing tracks but also influenced a wave of remixes across the genre.

The equation for their collaborative impact can be represented as:

$$I = C \times E \tag{45}$$

where I is influence, C is collaborations, and E is the exposure gained through those collaborations. This formula highlights how their partnerships amplify their reach and reinforce their status as trendsetters.

The Flosstradamus Effect

The influence of Flosstradamus extends beyond their own music. The duo has been instrumental in shaping the sound of emerging artists, often referred to as the *Flosstradamus Effect*. This phenomenon is observed when new artists adopt elements of their style, leading to a broader acceptance of trap and bass-heavy music within the EDM community.

For instance, the rise of artists like [?] and [?] can be traced back to the groundwork laid by Flosstradamus. Their willingness to experiment and push boundaries has inspired a new generation of musicians to explore similar sounds, thus perpetuating the cycle of innovation within the genre.

Conclusion

In conclusion, Flosstradamus has established themselves as trendsetters and taste makers in the EDM landscape through their innovative sound, strategic collaborations, and the influence they wield over emerging artists. Their journey reflects the dynamic nature of the music industry, where adaptability and creativity are paramount. As they continue to evolve, their role in shaping the future of EDM remains significant, leaving a lasting impact on both the genre and the artists that follow in their footsteps.

Reinventing Live Shows and Concert Experiences

In the ever-evolving landscape of electronic dance music (EDM), Flosstradamus has consistently pushed the envelope in reinventing live shows and concert experiences. The duo recognized early on that a mere performance was no longer sufficient to captivate audiences; instead, they sought to create immersive experiences that transcended traditional boundaries. This quest for innovation can be understood through several key theories and concepts in music performance and audience engagement.

The Theory of Immersive Experiences

At the core of Flosstradamus' approach lies the theory of immersive experiences, which posits that audience engagement is maximized when participants feel a deep connection to the performance. According to Pine and Gilmore (1998), the experience economy suggests that businesses must create memorable events that engage customers on multiple sensory levels. Flosstradamus embraced this theory by integrating visual elements, interactive technologies, and audience participation into their shows.

Multisensory Engagement

To enhance the sensory experience, Flosstradamus employed cutting-edge visual technology, including LED screens, laser displays, and synchronized light shows. These elements were not merely decorative but were intricately woven into the fabric of their performances. For instance, during their hit track "*Rollup*," the duo used a dynamic light display that responded to the beat, creating a visual representation of the music that enveloped the audience. This multisensory engagement aligns with the findings of Spence (2014), who emphasizes the importance of integrating sight and sound to create a holistic experience.

Audience Participation and Interaction

Flosstradamus also revolutionized live performances by incorporating audience participation. They invited fans on stage, engaged them through social media, and even encouraged them to contribute to live remixing during shows. This participatory approach not only democratized the performance but also fostered a sense of community among fans. As noted by Hennion (2001), this interaction transforms passive listeners into active participants, enhancing their emotional investment in the music.

Case Study: The *"Flosstradamus Experience"* Tour

A prime example of Flosstradamus' innovative approach is their "*Flosstradamus Experience*" tour. This tour featured a unique stage design that allowed for 360-degree viewing, enabling fans to experience the performance from multiple angles. The setlist was curated to include not only their greatest hits but also unexpected mashups and remixes, keeping the audience engaged and on their toes.

Moreover, the tour utilized augmented reality (AR) technology, allowing fans to interact with digital elements through their smartphones. This technological integration not only made the shows more engaging but also provided a platform for fans to share their experiences on social media, amplifying the reach of their performances.

Addressing Challenges

Despite the success of their innovative strategies, Flosstradamus faced challenges in maintaining the balance between technological integration and live performance authenticity. Critics argued that excessive reliance on technology could detract from the musicianship and emotional connection of live shows. To address this, the duo made a conscious effort to ensure that their performances remained rooted in live instrumentation and authentic sound. As a result, they began incorporating live musicians and vocalists into their shows, creating a hybrid experience that honored both the electronic roots and the organic essence of music.

Conclusion: A Lasting Impact

In conclusion, Flosstradamus' commitment to reinventing live shows and concert experiences has not only set them apart in the EDM scene but has also influenced a generation of artists seeking to create more engaging performances. By embracing immersive experiences, fostering audience participation, and addressing the challenges of technological integration, they have redefined what it means to perform live in the modern music landscape. As they continue to innovate, Flosstradamus remains a beacon of creativity and inspiration in the world of electronic music.

$$E = mc^2 \tag{46}$$

Where E represents the energy of the experience, m symbolizes audience engagement, and c denotes the creativity of the performance. This equation metaphorically illustrates the explosive potential of combining these elements to create unforgettable concert experiences.

Flosstradamus' Enduring Impact on the EDM Landscape

Flosstradamus, the dynamic duo that emerged from the vibrant streets of Chicago, has left an indelible mark on the EDM landscape. Their journey through the sonic realms of electronic music is not just a tale of personal success; it is a narrative that has shaped the very fabric of the genre itself. To understand their impact, we must delve into the various dimensions of their contributions, the challenges they faced, and the innovations they introduced.

The Trap Revolution

One of Flosstradamus' most significant contributions to the EDM landscape is their role in pioneering the trap genre. Trap music, characterized by its heavy bass, crisp snares, and syncopated hi-hats, found its way into the hearts of listeners largely due to the duo's innovative approach. Their mixtapes, particularly *TNGHT*, showcased a fusion of hip-hop and electronic elements, creating a sound that resonated with both EDM enthusiasts and hip-hop fans alike.

The equation that encapsulates their influence can be summarized as follows:

$$\text{Trap Popularity} \propto \text{Flosstradamus' Mixtapes} + \text{Collaborative Efforts} \quad (47)$$

This equation suggests that the popularity of trap music is directly proportional to the duo's mixtapes and their collaborations with other artists. Their remix of *Original Don* by *Flosstradamus* and *TNGHT* became anthems at festivals, further solidifying their status as trendsetters within the genre.

Innovative Live Performances

Flosstradamus has also revolutionized the live performance aspect of EDM. Their shows are not just concerts; they are immersive experiences that engage audiences on multiple levels. By incorporating live instruments, visual effects, and audience interaction, they have set a new standard for what a live EDM performance can entail.

The impact of their innovative performances can be quantified through audience engagement metrics, which include:

$$\text{Audience Engagement} = \frac{\text{Live Interaction} + \text{Visual Effects}}{\text{Standard Performance Elements}} \quad (48)$$

This formula highlights that audience engagement is enhanced when live interaction and visual effects are prioritized over traditional performance elements. Flosstradamus' ability to create a communal atmosphere at their shows has inspired countless artists to adopt similar strategies, thus reshaping the live EDM experience.

Mentorship and Influence

Beyond their music and performances, Flosstradamus has played a crucial role in mentoring the next generation of artists. By collaborating with emerging talents and providing platforms for them to showcase their work, they have fostered a sense of community within the EDM scene. This mentorship is vital for the continued evolution of the genre, as it ensures that fresh ideas and perspectives are constantly being introduced.

The impact of their mentorship can be expressed through the following relationship:

$$\text{Emerging Artists' Success} \propto \text{Flosstradamus' Mentorship} + \text{Collaborative Opportunitie} \tag{49}$$

This equation illustrates that the success of emerging artists is directly proportional to the mentorship provided by Flosstradamus and the collaborative opportunities they create. Artists like *Baauer* and *Dillon Francis* have cited Flosstradamus as influential figures in their careers, demonstrating the duo's ability to shape the future of EDM.

Cultural Impact and Legacy

Flosstradamus' influence extends beyond music; it encompasses cultural shifts within the EDM community. Their style, characterized by a blend of streetwear and festival fashion, has set trends that resonate with fans worldwide. This cultural impact can be analyzed through the following framework:

$$\text{Cultural Influence} = \text{Musical Innovation} + \text{Fashion Trends} + \text{Social Media Presence} \tag{50}$$

In this context, cultural influence is the result of a combination of musical innovation, fashion trends initiated by the duo, and their strategic use of social media to engage with fans. By effectively leveraging platforms like Instagram and Twitter, they have created a brand that transcends music, becoming cultural icons within the EDM scene.

Conclusion: An Enduring Legacy

In conclusion, Flosstradamus' enduring impact on the EDM landscape is a testament to their creativity, innovation, and dedication to the genre. Their pioneering work in trap music, revolutionary live performances, mentorship of emerging artists, and cultural influence have collectively redefined what it means to be a successful artist in the electronic music sphere. As they continue to evolve and inspire, their legacy will undoubtedly shape the future of EDM for years to come.

The echoes of their influence resonate throughout the music industry, reminding us that true artistry lies not only in personal success but in the ability to uplift and inspire others along the way.

Leaving a Lasting Legacy

The journey of Flosstradamus is not merely a timeline of events but a profound narrative that intertwines creativity, innovation, and the relentless pursuit of artistic expression. As they reflect on their trajectory, it becomes evident that their legacy transcends charts and accolades; it is about the indelible mark they have left on the electronic dance music (EDM) landscape and the generations of artists they have inspired.

At the heart of Flosstradamus' legacy is their pioneering role in the trap genre, a subgenre of hip-hop that they helped elevate within the EDM community. The duo's innovative sound, characterized by heavy basslines, syncopated hi-hats, and infectious melodies, has become a blueprint for countless artists. The equation of their influence can be summarized as:

$$\text{Legacy} = \text{Innovation} + \text{Influence} + \text{Inspiration}$$

Where: - **Innovation** refers to their unique sound and approach to music production. - **Influence** encompasses their collaborations and the artists they've inspired. - **Inspiration** highlights their role in mentoring and fostering new talent.

Mentoring Upcoming Artists

Flosstradamus has not only impacted the music they produce but has also taken on the role of mentors in the industry. They have established initiatives aimed at nurturing emerging artists, providing them with the tools and guidance necessary to navigate the complexities of the music business. This mentorship has manifested in various forms, from direct collaboration to hosting workshops and seminars that emphasize the importance of creativity, resilience, and adaptability.

For example, their collaboration with rising producers such as insert artist names has resulted in tracks that blend the distinctive Flosstradamus sound with fresh, innovative ideas. These partnerships serve as a testament to their commitment to fostering the next generation of musical talent.

The Flosstradamus Sound in Contemporary Music

The sonic fingerprints of Flosstradamus can be traced throughout contemporary music, as their influence extends beyond EDM into pop, hip-hop, and beyond. Their signature style has been adopted and adapted by numerous artists, creating a ripple effect that has reshaped the musical landscape. The integration of trap elements into mainstream music has led to a new era where genres are increasingly blurred, and collaborations are commonplace.

This phenomenon can be illustrated by examining the success of tracks such as insert popular tracks influenced by Flosstradamus, which feature production techniques reminiscent of Flosstradamus' early work. Their ability to push boundaries and redefine genre conventions has cemented their status as trendsetters in the industry.

Reinventing Live Shows and Concert Experiences

One of the most significant aspects of Flosstradamus' legacy lies in their revolutionary approach to live performances. They have redefined what it means to experience a concert, integrating cutting-edge technology, immersive visuals, and audience interaction to create unforgettable experiences. Their shows are not just concerts; they are communal celebrations of music and culture.

The use of dynamic stage setups, synchronized light displays, and live instrumentation has elevated their performances to new heights. This innovative approach has set a standard for live shows across genres, prompting other artists to rethink how they engage with their audiences. The equation for their live performance success can be expressed as:

$$\text{Live Experience} = \text{Innovation} \times \text{Engagement} \times \text{Visuals}$$

Where: - **Innovation** encompasses unique stage designs and technology. - **Engagement** refers to the connection fostered with the audience. - **Visuals** highlight the importance of aesthetics in enhancing the overall experience.

Flosstradamus as Trendsetters and Taste Makers

Flosstradamus' influence extends into the realm of cultural trends, where they have established themselves as tastemakers within the EDM community. Their ability to identify and promote emerging sounds and styles has positioned them at the forefront of the genre's evolution. By championing new artists and collaborating with diverse musicians, they have played a crucial role in shaping the musical direction of EDM.

The duo's keen sense of the industry's pulse allows them to stay ahead of the curve, ensuring that their music remains relevant and impactful. This adaptability is a key component of their legacy, demonstrating that true artistry lies in the willingness to evolve while remaining authentic to one's roots.

Leaving a Lasting Impact

Ultimately, the legacy of Flosstradamus is one of transformation, inspiration, and resilience. As they continue to create and innovate, their influence will undoubtedly resonate for years to come. The lessons learned from their journey—embracing change, nurturing talent, and redefining boundaries—serve as a guiding light for both established and aspiring artists alike.

In conclusion, Flosstradamus has not only left a lasting legacy in the EDM landscape but has also inspired a generation of musicians to push the envelope of creativity. Their story is a reminder that music is a powerful force that can unite, inspire, and transcend time. As they look to the future, the echoes of their journey will continue to inspire new waves of artists, ensuring that their impact endures long after the final beat fades.

Conclusion

Looking Back: The Journey of Flosstradamus

Lessons Learned and Milestones Achieved

The journey of Flosstradamus is not merely a tale of beats and rhythms; it is a rich tapestry woven with lessons learned, milestones achieved, and the occasional misstep that only serves to highlight the importance of resilience in the music industry. As they navigated the vast and often tumultuous waters of the EDM scene, Flosstradamus discovered several key insights that not only shaped their musical identity but also paved the way for future generations of artists.

The Importance of Authenticity

One of the most profound lessons Flosstradamus learned early on was the significance of authenticity in their music. In a world saturated with trends and fleeting fads, staying true to their roots became a cornerstone of their success. They realized that audiences resonate with genuine passion and creativity, leading them to cultivate a sound that reflects their unique experiences and influences. This authenticity not only attracted a loyal fan base but also set them apart in a crowded market.

Embracing Change and Evolution

As Flosstradamus evolved, they faced the inevitable challenge of change. The EDM landscape is notorious for its rapid shifts, and adapting to these changes became crucial. They learned that stagnation could lead to obsolescence. By embracing experimentation and innovation, they were able to pioneer the trap genre, which became a defining moment in their career. This willingness to evolve is encapsulated in the equation:

$$\text{Success} = \text{Authenticity} + \text{Adaptability}$$

This formula illustrates that while authenticity builds a strong foundation, adaptability ensures longevity in a dynamic industry.

Collaboration as a Catalyst for Growth

Another pivotal lesson was the power of collaboration. Throughout their journey, Flosstradamus engaged with various artists, each bringing their own flair to the table. These collaborations not only enriched their sound but also expanded their reach. For instance, their remix of *"Roll Up"* showcased how blending different styles can create something fresh and exciting. The synergy of diverse musical perspectives allowed them to tap into new audiences and explore uncharted territories in their music.

Navigating Fame and Personal Relationships

With success came the pressures of fame, which posed challenges that tested their personal and professional relationships. Flosstradamus learned that maintaining open communication and prioritizing their friendship was essential. They discovered that the equation:

$$\text{Sustained Success} = \text{Strong Relationships} + \text{Effective Communication}$$

held true. By fostering a supportive environment, they were able to navigate the complexities of fame without losing sight of their bond, allowing them to thrive both as individuals and as a duo.

The Value of Resilience

Perhaps the most significant lesson was the value of resilience. The road to success is often riddled with setbacks, and Flosstradamus faced their fair share of obstacles, from creative conflicts to external pressures. However, they learned that each challenge was an opportunity for growth. Their ability to bounce back from adversity is encapsulated in the phrase:

$$\text{Resilience} = \text{Challenge} + \text{Growth}$$

This mindset not only helped them overcome difficulties but also reinforced their commitment to their craft, leading to a successful reunion and a reinvigorated sound.

Milestones Achieved

Throughout their journey, Flosstradamus celebrated numerous milestones that marked their evolution as artists. From their early mixtapes that went viral, establishing them as pioneers of the trap genre, to headlining major music festivals worldwide, each achievement was a testament to their hard work and dedication. Notable milestones include:

+ **Viral Mixtapes:** Their early mixtapes, such as *"The Mixtape"*, garnered millions of streams, propelling them into the spotlight.

+ **Record Label Signing:** Signing with a prominent record label marked a significant turning point, allowing them to reach a broader audience.

+ **Festival Headliners:** Performing at major festivals like Coachella and Lollapalooza solidified their status as leading figures in the EDM scene.

+ **Innovative Collaborations:** Their collaborations with artists from various genres showcased their versatility and willingness to push boundaries.

These milestones not only reflect their achievements but also serve as reminders of the lessons learned along the way. Each step in their journey has contributed to the legacy of Flosstradamus, proving that success is not just about the destination but the experiences and lessons gathered along the way.

In conclusion, the story of Flosstradamus is a compelling narrative of growth, resilience, and the pursuit of authenticity. The lessons learned and milestones achieved are not just markers of their journey but also serve as inspiration for aspiring artists navigating the ever-changing landscape of the music industry. As they continue to evolve and influence the next generation, Flosstradamus stands as a testament to the power of music and the bonds that create it.

The Band's Enduring Friendship

Friendship is often described as the bedrock of collaboration in the music industry, and for Flosstradamus, this has proven to be an essential element of their success. The bond between Josh and Curt extends beyond mere musical partnership; it is a relationship built on shared experiences, mutual respect, and an unwavering commitment to their craft. This section delves into the dynamics of their friendship, exploring how it has shaped their journey and contributed to their enduring legacy.

The Foundation of Trust

At the heart of Flosstradamus' enduring friendship lies a foundation of trust. Trust is a critical component in any relationship, especially in the high-pressure environment of the music industry. According to social psychologist Robert C. Solomon, trust is a "willingness to be vulnerable" in the presence of another. For Josh and Curt, this vulnerability is evident in their willingness to share creative ideas, experiment with new sounds, and even confront challenges head-on.

$$T = \frac{V}{R} \tag{51}$$

Where T represents trust, V is vulnerability, and R is risk. In the context of their friendship, the equation illustrates that a higher level of vulnerability leads to greater trust, enabling them to navigate the complexities of fame and creativity together.

Shared Experiences

The journey of Flosstradamus has been filled with highs and lows, but it is the shared experiences that have solidified their friendship. From their early days in Chicago, where they bonded over hip-hop and electronic music, to their rise to fame, each milestone has been a testament to their partnership.

One notable example is their first major festival performance at Lollapalooza. The excitement and anxiety of stepping onto such a grand stage were palpable, yet they faced it together, encouraging one another. This moment not only marked a turning point in their careers but also reinforced their bond.

Navigating Challenges Together

No relationship is without its challenges, and Flosstradamus has faced their fair share. The pressures of fame, the expectations of their fans, and the inevitable creative differences have tested their friendship. However, the way they navigate these challenges has only strengthened their connection.

In moments of tension, they have employed open communication as a strategy for resolution. According to the theory of constructive conflict resolution, addressing issues directly can lead to stronger relationships. This approach is evident in how Josh and Curt have managed to maintain their friendship even during periods of hiatus and solo projects.

$$R = C + E \tag{52}$$

Where R represents relationship strength, C is communication, and E is empathy. By fostering effective communication and demonstrating empathy towards each other's individual journeys, they have cultivated a resilient friendship.

The Role of Humor

Humor is another vital ingredient in the recipe for their enduring friendship. In the words of comedian Steve Carell, "A good friend is someone who can make you laugh even in the most trying times." Josh and Curt often use humor to diffuse tension and keep their spirits high during challenging times. Their ability to laugh together has not only made the journey enjoyable but has also served as a coping mechanism during the rigors of touring and recording.

A Lifelong Bond

As Flosstradamus continues to evolve, their friendship remains a constant source of strength. The lessons learned from their journey together—trust, shared experiences, effective communication, and humor—are foundational elements that will guide them into the future.

In conclusion, the enduring friendship between Josh and Curt is a testament to the power of collaboration in the music industry. As they look back on their journey, it is clear that their bond has been instrumental in shaping who they are as artists and as friends. Their story serves as an inspiring reminder that at the core of every successful partnership lies a deep-rooted friendship that can weather any storm.

Beyond the Echoes: The Legacy of Flosstradamus

The legacy of Flosstradamus is a vibrant tapestry woven from the threads of creativity, innovation, and community. As pioneers in the electronic dance music (EDM) scene, they not only shaped their own musical paths but also influenced an entire generation of artists and fans. Their journey, marked by a series of groundbreaking milestones, serves as a testament to the power of collaboration and the relentless pursuit of artistic expression.

Cultural Impact and Influence

Flosstradamus emerged from the underground Chicago music scene, a city known for its rich musical heritage. Their unique sound, characterized by a fusion of trap, hip-hop, and electronic music, resonated with audiences far beyond their hometown. The duo's ability to blend genres not only set them apart but also paved the way for a new wave of artists who sought to experiment with sound. This genre-blending approach can be analyzed through the lens of cultural theory, particularly the concept of *intertextuality*, where the meaning of a piece is shaped by its relationship to other texts and genres.

The success of their mixtapes, particularly the viral sensation *TNGHT*, exemplifies this intertextuality. By incorporating elements from various musical traditions, Flosstradamus created a sound that was both familiar and fresh, attracting a diverse fanbase. Their influence is evident in the works of contemporary artists who cite them as inspirations, thus perpetuating their legacy within the evolving landscape of EDM.

Mentorship and Community Building

Beyond their musical contributions, Flosstradamus has played a significant role in mentoring upcoming artists. This aspect of their legacy is critical, as it highlights the importance of community in the music industry. By providing platforms for emerging talent, they have fostered a supportive environment that encourages creativity and collaboration. The duo's commitment to nurturing the next generation is reminiscent of the *social capital theory*, which posits that social networks have value and can facilitate cooperation for mutual benefit.

For instance, their collaborations with lesser-known artists have not only elevated those individuals but also enriched the Flosstradamus sound. This reciprocal relationship exemplifies how legacy is built not just through individual success but through the success of others. The impact of these mentorships can be seen in the rising popularity of artists who have been influenced by Flosstradamus, further solidifying their status as industry leaders.

Innovations in Live Performance

Flosstradamus has also left an indelible mark on live performance within the EDM scene. Their innovative approach to concerts—integrating live instruments, multimedia visuals, and interactive elements—has redefined the concert experience. This evolution can be analyzed through the theory of *experiential marketing*, which emphasizes creating memorable experiences that engage the audience on multiple sensory levels.

By pushing the boundaries of what a live show can be, Flosstradamus has set new standards for performance artistry. Their ability to connect with audiences through high-energy sets and immersive experiences has inspired countless artists to rethink their own approaches to live performances. This legacy of innovation is a critical component of their overall impact on the EDM landscape.

Enduring Friendship and Artistic Integrity

At the heart of Flosstradamus' legacy is the enduring friendship between Josh and Curt. Their ability to navigate the complexities of fame and personal challenges while maintaining a strong bond is a powerful narrative that resonates with fans. This aspect of their journey speaks to the importance of *emotional intelligence* in collaborative endeavors, as they have demonstrated the ability to communicate openly and support each other through thick and thin.

The duo's commitment to artistic integrity is another cornerstone of their legacy. In an industry often driven by commercial success, Flosstradamus has remained true to their roots, continually exploring new sounds and ideas. This dedication to authenticity not only enriches their music but also inspires others to pursue their artistic visions without compromise.

Conclusion: A Legacy That Echoes

As we reflect on the legacy of Flosstradamus, it becomes clear that their impact extends far beyond the music itself. They have shaped the EDM landscape, influenced countless artists, and built a community that celebrates creativity and collaboration. Their story is a reminder that true legacy is not just about personal achievements but about the connections we forge and the lives we touch along the way.

In conclusion, the echoes of Flosstradamus will continue to resonate in the music world, inspiring future generations to push boundaries, embrace collaboration, and above all, stay true to their artistic selves. Their journey, marked by innovation, mentorship, and friendship, is a legacy that will endure, reminding us all of the transformative power of music.

Index

Milton Keynes UK
Ingram Content Group UK Ltd.
UKHW022127051124
450708UK00015B/1214